Praise for Etel Adnan

"A meditative heir to Nietzsch[e] and the verses of Sufi mystic[s]... reflections on pain and beauty"

BENJ[AMIN SCHNEI]DER, *New York Times*

"An iconic Lebanese-American cultural figure."

NANA ASFOUR, *Paris Review*

"Her writing is as fiercely complex and political as her paintings are serenely spare and personal."

KAELEN WILSON-GOLDIE, *Frieze*

"It must be evident to anyone even slightly aware of Etel Adnan's career that her work exhibits formidable intellectual and creative range. Adnan has refused to be bound by the constraints of nation, gender, genre, medium, or discipline, in order to venture into explorations of social, political, imagined, and aesthetic surfaces and sites. Over the years she has been saddened by the prevalence of suffering, and she has always been intolerant of stupidity. But at its core, her work is a manifestation of an enduring will to life and an impassioned capacity for joy."

LYN HEJINIAN

"Arguably the most celebrated and accomplished Arab American author writing today."

MELUS: *Multi-Ethnic Literature of the United States*

"Etel Adnan is a beacon of thought in a disrempt world. In her writing, I sense her hovering just beyond, in view but ungraspable, yet grounding me in ever changing realization: luminous company, trusted guide, necessary source of immediate information. Adnan is a visionary of the meteoric and diasporic. Oscillating between the ecstatic and the unbearable, she finds home in the evasive emplacements of each moment."

CHARLES BERNSTEIN

"Adnan's work is the anti-Oxymandias—a corrective to exuberant art-world bling. There is none of the bravado or self-regarding mythologizing of other artists of her stature."

NEGAR AZIMI, *Wall Street Journal Magazine*

"In *The Heart of the Heart of the Country* is a gorgeously, multi-layered prose poem/poetic essay which represents a journey through the 20th century. Adnan, who has been consciously present for most of the historical disasters of that century as well as its many experimental literary movements, has tuned her language to an indelible pitch that is by turns lyrical, quizzical, wistful, and wise."

KIM JENSEN, *Rain Taxi*

"*Night* is in equal measure a series of meditations on intersubjectivity and spirituality, and a dialogue between prose poetry and short verse."

MATT TURNER, *Hyperallergic*

"In the long dramatic poem entitled 'The Arab Apocalypse,' Etel Adnan draws a huge mixed media canvas where she fuses poetry, painting, and music to create her own 'Guernica'...."

MONA TAKIEDDINE AMYUNI, *Al Jadid*

"Etel Adnan is a world treasure whom more of the world needs to know. Her poetry, her visual art, her longstanding feminist vision—a philosophical poethics of rage transmuted into love and vice versa—is crucial to the kinds of creative generosity that must replace our geopolitical cordoning off of the disasters of 'others.'"

JOAN RETALLACK

"With ever-increasing wisdom and clarity, Etel Adnan's work continues to illuminate the human condition. From the very distant past to the all-consuming present, she has found ways to condense intellect and emotion into surprising forms that enact the dance towards freedom."

AMMIEL ALCALAY

"Etel Adnan's powerful writing and artwork is a startling combination of the poetic and political. Her small paintings with their intense colors, forceful rhythms, and built-up abstract shapes echo real and imaginary landscapes. They evoke the forces that form her life: a love of place, a distinct voice, and a sensuous presence. Her accordion books with texts in Arabic and other scripts emphasize the role of calligraphy and drawing in shaping her voice. Adnan's work is a rare instance of strong interconnected work in both writing and painting."

SUSAN BEE

"*To look at the sea is to become what one is: An Etel Adnan Reader* is a milestone and a monument: a milestone for the ongoing recognition of a writer who, despite her prescience, relevance, and power, has remained marginal for many American readers."

LINDSAY TURNER, *Kenyon Review*

"Her jubilant use of color runs throughout the works and places her in a lineage of artists including Sonia Delaunay and Paul Klee."

ELIZABETH FULLERTON, *Art in America*

"Etel Adnan is a force. I share paint with her and she shares wisdom and honesty. Her paintings are colorful and free, with a visual intelligence few can match. Her writing is profound and will not yield easily. It has a pure but darker side, demanding and expecting truthful attention, offering up the poetic. And there is another kind of color and materiality—both strong and tender."

NANCY HAYNES

"Nostalgic and meanderingly autobiographical, these powerful emotional tales seem almost magically wrought, offering a flavor of the author's own vast experience and travels."

On *Master of the Eclipse, Publishers Weekly*

"*Surge*, as the title suggests, is a book awash in movement: the movement of mind, of time and of memory."

IAN MALENEY, *The Irish Times*

THE PERFORMANCE IDEAS SERIES

PERFORMANCE IDEAS explores performance that crosses boundaries of all live art forms and media. The series highlights the long-standing editorial commitment of PAJ Publications to bring together the histories of performance in theatre and in visual art for a more expansive vision of artistic practice.

OTHER BOOKS IN THIS SERIES

The Sun
on the Tongue

ETEL ADNAN

Edited by **Bonnie Marranca** and **Klaudia Ruschkowski**

New York, New York

Published by PAJ Publications, P.O. Box 532, Village Station, New York, NY 10014.

PAJ Publications is distributed to the trade by Consortium Book Sales and Distribution: www.cbsd.com

Publisher of PAJ Publications: Bonnie Marranca

First Edition. Printed on acid-free paper.

Library of Congress Cataloging-in-Publication Data

Names: Adnan, Etel, author. | Marranca, Bonnie, editor. | Ruschkowski, Klaudia, editor.

Title: The sun on the tongue / Etel Adnan ; Bonnie Marranca and Klaudia Ruschkowski (editors).

Description: New York, NY : PAJ Publications, 2018. | Series: The performance ideas series

Identifiers: LCCN 2018018756 | ISBN 9781555541651 (alk. paper)

Classification: LCC PS3551.D65 A6 2018 | DDC 818/.5409—dc23

LC record available at https://lccn.loc.gov/2018018756

Contents

Untitled, 1970–73. Ink on paper

A Woman, A World

BONNIE MARRANCA

Etel Adnan arrived in Paris to start a new life a few years before Albert Camus was to die. What links them is more than the fact that she now lives in his former apartment building. It has rather to do with their origins in the Arab world and status as outsiders to French culture, which imparted to each one an acute understanding of what it means to be fully human. Under such conditions individual consciousness unfolds in a high state of attentiveness, and one can only create dangerously.

In her "Short Letter to a Young Poet" that opens this volume, Adnan affirms it is a matter of life and death to write poetry, and, at its end, in the excerpt from *There*, one of my favorites among her writings, one has only to follow the centrifugal force of her thoughts as they turn from self to other. Who is she? Where is she? Here? Over there? I am reminded of Merce Cunningham's description of his dance as having no fixed points in space. Wherever you are is a center. That's how I perceive Etel Adnan's prolific art-making through the changing climates in which she is now poet, painter, essayist, philosopher, and now journalist, novelist, memoirist. When I first became acquainted with her writing I wondered if I might be lost in its immensity of mind, something I had considered previously with Gertrude Stein, another writer whose spirit is housed in the same Saint-Sulpice neighborhood. But Adnan

9

knows how to temper the weight of the world with a lightness and freedom that humble artists possess. Perhaps that is because, as she herself reveals, she has spent a lifetime in the company of angels, Paul Klee having been one of them.

Profoundly humanist, you can tell she loves being in the world, the soulfulness of her phrasing illuminated in the lyrical reflections of a painter's palette. She notices everything, her observations defined not merely by looking but a looking into, the manner of an artist possessed of a sense of wonder that has never left her. Ordinary life is given the value of myth and cosmic event or sometimes it is just ordinary life in all its fundamental lessons. There is a true goodness in her spirit that comes forth in a deeply compassionate feeling for people and suffering that is not always evident in exceptional thinkers. She has a philosophic mind that avoids detachment through analytical prowess, unflinching in its recognition of evil, shame, horror, and violence in all their manifestations. This comprehension of life extends from the ancient world to the contemporary world, to all species and to outer space.

And still, the cosmopolitan in Adnan celebrates her great pleasures in life: love, art, travel, food, conversation, weather. She evinces a mystical attachment to nature, reveling in her beloved Mt. Tamalpais of the California years, or recalling the experience of swimming in the sea in Beirut. Showing her humorous side, she compares her method for starting each new book with the image of a bird waiting for an airstream and then just going with the flow. In Adnan's great body of work is the portrait of a person who has experienced true happiness. A woman who loves music. She imagines life as a rose and thinking as a form of poetry, an inkwell as a *commedia* figure. What is her intriguing title "the sun on the tongue" but an image of light warming the intimate floor on which one stages speaking, tasting, caressing? Perhaps this is the true meaning of luminosity.

Born in Lebanon, in 1925, to a Greek mother and a Syrian father, Adnan has lived the idea of worldliness in the long decades between leaving Beirut in the late nineteen-forties, settling many years in California, and moving permanently to Paris in the twenty-first century, crisscrossing multiple cultures and continents that experienced fierce conflicts over myth and history through war, exile, diaspora, colonization, and that yet have produced everywhere glorious poetry and heartbreakingly beautiful images and friendships. Her feeling for geography is spiritual. There is World War II and then there is the revolution of Pina Bausch; there is the Lebanese Civil War and then there is her remarkable heroine Marie-Rose; there is the Iraq War and then there is the legacy of al-Hallaj. The freedom of women exists alongside terrible crimes of honor.

Her dreams of Mayakovsky float between Moscow and North Beach. An abstract landscape is the color of memory. Her love poems make a songbook. Love and its passions is a constant theme. What she writes about Nietzsche in *The Cost for Love* might just as well be attributed to her: that he had no system but a series of intuitions borne out of the generosity of his mind, this generosity being a form of love. Risk everything.

In the world of Adnan wisdom is the better part of virtuosity, whatever shape it takes: writings, paintings, plays, drawings, tapestries, films, artist's books, essays on art, literature, dance, and theatre. The memoir is her natural home because it is a form of journey that tells stories about the lives of real people and places, weaving in and out of memory through aphoristic fragments and circuitous pathways. Just as comfortable a setting is the unfolding of her beloved accordion-like *leporello* that is essentially a form of narrative in motion. Here the lines of writing and drawing and poetry fill the bellowing pages of a book that opens wider and wider into time and space.

In a moment of serious whimsy, some years ago Etel Adnan confided in one of the jewel-like paragraphs that distinguish her writings, "I have to tell you: I am, each year, a year older. But there is a place in an anti-universe where I am, each year, a year younger."

O, lady of Rue Madame, what new knowledge can you reveal to Earth's anxious souls between here and eternity?

Short Letter to a Young Poet

My dear Friend,

A letter to a poet is necessarily to be a love letter. And if one has to speak of poetry one is walking by the edge of the sea. Or on a rope. On unstable grounds. So we are going to deal, from the start, with feelings and uncertainties.

You want to be a poet. You say you don't know what it means to be a poet or how to go about it. And it's just as well. No poet has ever known the real reason for wanting to be such an unconventional person. In some ways, it may look simple. You stumble on a little stone or you take a pencil, open a page on your computer, you align words and they take off. They seem to have no other purpose than to be aligned, but you are the only one to know that at that very moment you have put your life on the line, not metaphorically, but in a kind of tragic honesty.

I went a bit fast and spoke of tragedy, yes, poetry turns around tragedy. The desire to be a poet means that you are ready to deal with feelings, with intangible matters, to invite the invisible in the midst of a dinner, to see ghosts, where there are none, and to sleep only when you feel sleepy and not because of the hour. To be a poet often means to be available at odd hours to follow your spirit all the way into an abyss, to be fearless, to be curious about undefined objects, to never know where you are going and what may open you up to great dangers. It's dangerous that one says go to poetry because it may induce you to be bored with the limits of your own brain, and you may want to punch holes into the walls of those limits and to go beyond them and never come back. Thus, the life in poetry is a life of no return. It becomes a destiny. That is what is meant by tragedy here.

There is something obvious about it. It will be as if the gods took hold of you. You are endowed with the responsibility of your own making that looks inevitable. This is why so many poets have been flattered to be accused of being cursed. Cursed with a vision or a power, who knows.

But there is something special in there that arrests people's attention, that creates multiple layers of expectation, admiration, fear, or hostility that makes the lives of poets and artists as hard as they are.

You don't need to read too many books of poetry to come closer to the heart of poetry, but you need to love a few poets madly, love them more than yourself, for sure, but also more than any person or living thing. Valéry once said to Mallarmé that there was in every village of France a young person ready to die for him. I suppose for even a single line from Mallarmé.

That is utterly true. I remember sitting on the sidewalks of Beirut at age twenty and reading Baudelaire and becoming impervious to the traffic, to the people walking almost on my toes, even to the rain and the hour. For a long while I loved only two things: the sea and a couple of poets. And that stayed. If there is a paradise, they will be with me.

You will often hear someone say something like "politics doesn't make good poetry." But that's wrong. There is the *Iliad*, a political poem, a historical poem, here and there an intimate poem. It is not the subject matter that makes the poem, but how much that subject matter becomes a question of life and death for you, and how much you can manage, maybe more by instinct than by skill, to convey that experience. There are no certitudes in the world of the mind. It is a world of changing shadows, of overlapping shadows. So it is perhaps good to worry and not to worry at the same time, because doubt will always be there. Doubting is a way to say that there are no answers, for answers are often dangerous and become obstacles, dead ends. And anyway, reality is fluent in its essence.

A poet is not a special person. He or she is rather more of a person like all the others than one knows. I think that a poet should not pass judgment on himself endlessly, nor be too prone to self-censorship but should remain open. If you have the urge to kill, it's good to admit that desire and go into it, and search for where it comes from, what it entails, so it will be better not to actually kill anybody. It is good to enter the range of human possibility to admit that so many people we may despise keep hold of worlds of a complexity that we would never know if we did not remain open to them as much as we can.

The outside world and the inner world are each infinite. Let's start by realizing that immensity and let us get lost in it. One has to take the risk of getting lost, if one wants to find anything in any worlds.

To know is not a matter of accumulation, but of intensity, it is a matter of coming as close to the fire as one can, to burn. And you can burn by covering miles as you can burn in the obscurity of your room. In that inner journey, which has no bottom. Anyway you are going to be all alone in the most important moment of your life.

No advice will do, no instruction. Because every life is totally solitary and unlike anything else, once things get serious. So there is no advice to a young poet. It is his or her love for it, need for it. The resolution to try to do it—that will open the way. The thinking will come after. Write it down and leave it there and then we will see. There are no final texts. Do it. And then the others agree or disagree on the merits of what you have done. Be sensitive to what they say but remain the ultimate master of your work without being a judge. The best thing would be to let go. There is always another poem that will ask to be written.

I don't know exactly why, but I feel the urge of talking to you about happiness. We started with a recollection that people expect poets to be cursed. But I believe that poetry like great art springs from our deep reservoir of happiness. The subject matter may be somber, but the energy to express it is always a sign of life. Love is involved here. The capacity for love, the presence of love—love, when everything is said, is the most fundamental and the most difficult of all things human.

In the same vein I would like to confide in you that the thing that I miss most in our world is innocence. We are in a civilization (or lack of civilization) where innocence under all its forms has been lost. The planet has lost its innocence: it's all charted, mapped, owned—deserts and oceans included. Politicians don't even know what the word means. People are so filled with ready-made thoughts and beliefs that what they think has become rather meaningless.

Children are so over-educated, beginning at age two, that they will never be children. So what's left? What's left are the poets and the artists. They are the most important beings in the universe. Not those who just write poems and create artworks, but those who are poets, to start with. What we can truly call poetry starts with innocence. To be true to oneself is the starting point. To be fresh to the world is the starting point. Then life will take care. Nobody knows, until it happens, what will happen, so let go, at least don't ever lie, most of all to yourself. If the death of a fly touches you more than the death of a soldier let that go on a page. It will be your first poem.

We can go on, dear poet, but that's enough for today.

Thinking as a Form of Poetry

Etel Adnan in conversation with Klaudia Ruschkowski

Several conversations took place in San Gimignano, 2013, and in Paris, 2011/2016/2017.

Wittgenstein's "Whereof one cannot speak, thereof must one be silent" was answered by Pasolini with "Whereof one cannot speak, thereof one should write a poem."

I think Pasolini said something very right. Why do we have poetry? And it's not new, on the contrary, it's the oldest art in all of civilization, even before painting. Poetry—and also dance and singing—is a very basic art. You don't express functional things only, no, you want to express things that are almost impossible to say. So we say it in poetry. Now what do we mean by poetry? Basically, we don't know. We just do it. It's what we write when we are in a special state of mind. Not in the ordinary state of mind, when we stop and think. We want to put into words information connected closely with emotion, with thinking.

You said that poetry is like an impulse, you don't decide to sit and write down your thoughts, they really come over you.

That's it. I don't write poetry like: I sit down and now I'm going to write a poem. No. It's a mixture, many things come together in one sentence and I spit it out, I write it immediately because if I wait, sometimes only one or two minutes, I lose it. Poetry is impulsive, you can't write poems all the time. Poetry is urgent. You have to catch that thought, that line, that sentence which not only says things but expresses what you think about them, how you experience them, or speaks about something else that suddenly appears. Like Heidegger says: "Reality comes to the surface." What you say in poetry seems to emerge almost on its own, you don't fabricate it.

Your poetry has no special form, no rhyme, it has its own flow. It seems to me a kind of meditation.

Of course, there are many approaches and they all are culturally induced. Today one doesn't write with rhymes. Not that it's bad, there is great poetry with rhyme, sometimes even the best. Rhyme was meant to memorize, and today we don't memorize anymore, we read. Therefore, we don't need rhymes. Rhymes were used in theatre to memorize the texts more easily. Rhyme has its own beauty and repetition, but we can do repetition without it. Today we more and more write in free form so that poetry becomes not a style but the essence, this something special that you don't say all the time. Even simple things like "a piece of bread is on the table"—now, this can be poetry. You see, it's very strange, it depends when you say it and how, it depends on the context, even if it is autonomous, even if you say it alone.

Poetry as a special form of perception.

Yes. Poetry originates through perception and is really about perception. Something that's another aspect of poetry that is part of your everyday life. Two people can read the same line, one will say: it's poetry, and the other: no, it's just information. Sure, it's information in both cases, but there are different responses. Suddenly you see a piece of bread on a table. And you see it like a picture by Magritte or by Dalí, it's the same as the apples in Cézanne. Poetry isolates something and makes it mysterious.

Poetry, yes, but also painting, and in your case philosophy. There seems to me a mixture of all of them. When you are painting or drawing you're doing poetry and also philosophy, when you are writing a poem it's also a kind of painting and philosophical reflection.

Remember that in Europe, since Nietzsche, philosophy—what we call philosophy—has changed. Nietzsche was a great poet. Not when he wrote poems. But every book of his is also poetry. When you read *Ecce Homo*, you realize that it's a lyrical piece, it's philosophy. The boundary between poetry and philosophy has been erased to a great degree. Why? Because of the subject matter. Poetry used to speak of nature, it described nature or expressed love, anger, emotion. But why shouldn't poetry express ideas? In this case, it becomes poetry and philosophy at the same time.

There's a new poetry today where more and more people consider thinking as a form of poetry.

Like, let's say, Wittgenstein. Wittgenstein is a philosopher, a mathematician, and he had the greatest influence on poets these last thirty years. We have discovered that thinking triggers the same reaction that we ascribe to the creative power of poetry, to what we used to say poetry creates.

That would mean that poetry is the core of everything, of every artistic expression, but also of ideas and concepts in everyday life. Even more, the bridge between reality and non-reality.

That's how we get to this point. Any subject matter can be poetry, if you decide it is. So let's go back to what poetry means. As I said: a piece of bread on the table, we have it every day—and suddenly it's an epiphany. The piece of bread becomes mysterious. Because it is mysterious. Everything is mysterious. But we don't take time to see that. When we take the time to look at something, that something becomes a poetic object or a poetic feeling or a poetic thought.

In Seasons *you write about the weather. Does the weather have a poetic quality?*

I think weather is a most poetic element. We are nearly swimming in weather, weather is the air around us. We are in weather like we are in the sea when we swim, like a fish is in the water. Like an airplane is in the air, or a bird. The weather affects us because there is always some weather. Even when we don't feel the weather, it's there, we don't feel it because it is a certain condition. I love the weather. As a child, when suddenly winter arrived, it was always a big phenomenon. You see, we didn't have many toys in Lebanon, in my generation, when I grew up, and they were hidden. My mother only brought them out for a few days a year, around Christmas and New Year, so they shouldn't break. We didn't have radio, we didn't have television. We had nothing but the simplest daily life: go to school, come back, eat, sleep, see people who came to visit. That was our world. I am sure that it still exists today in villages in India or Africa, or even around the Mediterranean. The children, and also the adults, got so much out of what was just there. If there is no TV, well, a shadow on the wall becomes as important as a TV image. You perceive the world around you. That made me see the beauty and the meaning of the simple, ordinary things, I grew up with them. I had no brothers and sisters, no children to play with. So my life was about my immediate surroundings. The weather was a big happening.

Your toys, the things you've been thinking about, were the clouds, the plants, the sunsets, the sea.

You see, I didn't need to go to the museum, but the passage of a cloud that runs across the sky, I could watch for hours. And when the rain came. Your body changes, your skin, you feel differently. Then the summer came, we started to perspire and my parents said: We have to go to the mountains. Sometimes we couldn't go, but if we went then I came from a hot Beirut to the cool mountains. Do you see that we are like fish in water? Our whole body feels the weather. If we pay attention, it's an extraordinary thing.

In Seasons *you don't just talk about the weather as a phenome-non, you speak of mental and emotional states, of thinking and of feeling. You associate all this with the weather.*

I didn't want to describe the weather per se: hot, cold, ninety degrees, zero. I wanted to write a poem, to make a poem out of it, I was aware of that. A combination of the desire to think about the weather and to write a poem. So I wrote about the weather but I also wanted to write about the mind that perceives the weather, and other things, too. These are the last years of my life. My poetry has always been very political because of the many problems that exist. It was different than now. For the past seven or eight years, I've been trying to capture consciousness, to write about the mind in the very moment in which it works.

You explicitly wrote about phenomena of nature, for example, about fog. How did you decide on that idea?

The idea for a poem about fog has to do with the Bay Area around San Francisco. I lived there for fifty years. Every summer, in the middle of summer, there is fog, a special phenomenon because the interior of California is very dry and hot, but the ocean has a different temperature. On the coast where I lived, fog is spreading. It creates huge fog fields. When you cross the Golden Gate Bridge, you are in a fog, like in the classical Chinese paintings. Waves of fog, coming through the Golden Gate, and going all the way to Berkeley. So where I was, in Sausalito, the fog makes a wall, you don't see San Francisco any more. The entire landscape is as if it is under snow. Snow changes the landscape, but fog even more—it erases the landscape. You move like in a cloud. If you are traveling by car, you need the headlights during the day, because you don't see the road. That happens every year.

It's very dramatic. It's an extraordinary natural phenomenon. I'm fascinated by the real fog, but also what fog means to the mind. We are in a fog. Which doesn't mean that we are lost, that we are unhappy. We are in a new land. It's a new territory in the middle of a territory that you think you know. It's the same with night. Night also changes the landscape, takes it away, erases it. But fog is different from night because you see it come, like an object moving, like an animal, a cosmic animal walking on the hills and on the houses. I lived with this phenomenon, I waited for it every year, and suddenly I started writing a poem.

In your poetry the elements are often also philosophical concepts. Your poetry is always, in a sense, philosophy.

I studied philosophy. I never did my PhD. But I love Nietzsche. Nietzsche destroyed our faith in classical philosophy. He was right. We're not interested in the truth. There is no truth. That's relative. But thinking still exists. It was Heidegger who made it clear that Hölderlin was maybe more of a philosopher than Leibniz. You couldn't say that before. But that type of philosophy I agree with. Open philosophy. It's not important to contradict yourself or not, or what you are looking for. What I am looking for is what's called a poem. The mind doesn't work in a linear way like a theorem. It doesn't work as if we were writing a novel, which means to make choices. When we don't think about it, our thinking goes in all directions at the same time. I look at you and the word "New York," just now, crossed my mind. Why? No reason.

So if I want to write a poem about this instinct, I can write a poem and describe you. I can write a poem and think about a precise event. But I can also write about the moment in which it really happens. What happens? I see you, I see the color of your sweater, I see a page and a pencil and then, suddenly, the word "New York" came through, and now the word "shadow." I don't know why. I can write all this down, just as it happens, and I will call that a poem. I am working in this manner. I don't do it from morning to night, I'd go crazy, but there are special moments where I am like a double person. I let things happen, and I watch them as they happen. It's very exciting to write this kind of poetry.

Last night I read your Conversations with My Soul *and thought about how you often write conversations with yourself, that you simultaneously lead from the inside and yet perceive from the outside, as if another person.*

I think what you just said is what art is about. Art is created in moments when you are yourself and you control yourself. A moment of art is when Cézanne looks at an apple, he is aware that the apple is an object on its own, he cannot copy the apple a hundred per cent, it's a three-dimensional object. A painter cannot put it on canvas, canvas is flat, but he knows that he is drawing an apple, in his case as close as possible to the sensation that a real apple arouses, and he knows he is a painter, that he does something special. He is not fooling around, he is not getting ready to eat the apple. He is dialoguing with the apple and with himself.

> *What does that mean for your painting? Your paintings are often opaque, the color covers them completely, even in thick layers. Your drawings are incredibly open and flowing, wave movements.*

Everyone has their own way, thank God, these are not things you can define once and for all. As soon as you define them, they are already beginning to change, to you and to other people. You have to be careful. In that sense, it's a mystical experience like that of believers who want to reach God and never feel they succeed. The painter, what is he running after? We know that Rembrandt was running after his portrait, after the portraits of people but, of course, through the portrait he goes beyond. Instead of reaching God he reaches the essence of Man or of his own being in his self-portraits. He will never reach a hundred per cent, that's why he keeps doing it again. When I do paintings, I work with the palette knife and use oil paint. You see, there is also a dialogue with the objects you use. If you use a brush you work differently than when you use a palette knife or a pencil. When I use a palette knife, I apply large areas of the same color. If I use a brush and watercolors, then the material is freer, also my hand is freer and the result is a different one. When I use ink, which I really enjoy, I follow the trail of the brush. Often I don't know where this leads me.

I never know where I go with art because I don't work on a strict model. I don't work on a particular landscape. I work with the *idea* of landscape. This is very different. A landscape is also a power game, forces make a landscape. One hill appears on your right, another one goes up, the third one runs down, that's a way of perception because the hills are there. But we see them as a battle of different energies. That's how I see a landscape, and when I paint, I collect and capture different energies through different colors and shapes, and I do that instinctively. You don't know the result unless you see it. When I apply ink to paper, I follow it there, I bend the line, and I see a new line and I have no idea where the other line is going. The third line then takes on a relationship, so that the painting is at each moment a complex thing. You can leave it like that, but you can also say it still does not mean anything, and then you keep working.

When I follow what you say, it feels like something in you is determined from the beginning. The way of looking at the outside, the landscape, the weather, the surroundings, everything seems to come from a deep solitude, a loneliness that is nevertheless at home in the world, and in that you create yourself in a poetic moment and through your perception.

That's very nice, maybe you're right. Somebody who works is always alone. You're always alone, even when you cook. When you do something, you're alone with what you do. Isn't that true? That moment of loneliness is indispensable for things to happen. You are not imprisoned. You are alone—it's a kind of freedom. You have space in front of you. The world comes to you. I like the idea that the world collaborates with us, it's your idea of dialogue, a way to make that clear. Things influence us. Even when you pick up a brush or a pencil, a new world opens up to you. The brush opens worlds that are closed to the pencil. The pencil opens others. We call them possibilities, but they are worlds.

Don't you think that the society in which we live, surrounded by information, images, music, street life, noise, gives us little opportunity to be really alone? You come home, the TV is on, you are constantly bombarded with all sorts of information, you are constantly being informed about things that may be completely unnecessary. What does this development of infor-mation, speed, and technology mean for art, for poetry?

It's a question of balance. Too much information becomes zero information. The mind has its own tempo, its own rhythm. When the rhythm of the world outside does not correspond to your rhythm you stop, you are jammed. Information is good if you absorb it and do something with it. What we call informa-tion is not information, it's propaganda. You are not told some-thing because you should think. You are told something to stop you thinking. You are fed information that doesn't offer pos-sibilities of discussion. This is why we know so much and we know very little. We are bombarded. It's like eating too much. Then you are ill. So much information tires, numbs, and you become insensitive. The information will not be tracked down. They tell you something happened and then they don't tell you what happened next. So you don't really know much because you have the beginning of a story and you don't have the end. In addition, everything is communicated that your emotions can't corroborate, they can't follow, it goes too fast. It says: Somebody was killed and then immediately—buy shoes, it's good for you.

We live in a very dangerous moment because technology is getting so powerful. We can get to a point quickly where there are machines that read your mind when you walk in the street. What do you do then? Technology is good and bad, like everything else. In some cases it helps, there's a great potential but at the same time current danger. Who is going to control all that? We don't know where we are going. I'm afraid the human race could become so intelligent that it erases itself. I don't think it will happen in our lifetime, but the possibility exists. So we live in a very scared world, and art and poetry address that. Politicians should address it, but they don't. So it is with the rebels, the writers, the artists. The others are not insensitive but they are stunned. Very few people have the energy to think seriously about those things. You see, life is always between freedom and control, even in art.

In your work waves play a special role. The sea and waves. Waves of water, but also waves of energy, of sound or light.

Virginia Woolf wrote a book called *The Waves*, an experimental novel that's very poetic, and each chapter starts with a prose poem on the sea. A very beautiful book and very sensitive. It's a bit like the weather, people tremble. When there is a storm,

I get excited. I need weather, I get bored without the weather.
I like to climb mountains when the wind hits you. I like fog,
cloudy weather, I really do. I like mountains, to look at them,
also because of the climate change you notice while watching.
I like climate. That's how it started. When I read *The Waves*, in
1952, I was deeply impressed. Then I read it in a French trans-
lation by Marguerite Yourcenar, really extraordinary. I didn't
know that books like this existed. So it's a very important book
for me.

> *Besides waves and the sea, mountains are important to you and*
> *the sun and moon, clouds and wind, the ocean. Ocean and*
> *sea—are these just two different words for phenomena, or is*
> *there a difference of feeling for you?*

I don't know. But if we have two words there must be some
difference. It also depends of which sea we speak. I haven't seen
the Black Sea yet, but I would have loved to do that, including
the Caspian Sea. I know the Mediterranean and it's true that the
borders of the Mediterranean evoke a different feeling. Maybe
that's different when you're in the middle of the sea. Maybe
sailors, who spent their life out there, know that. But I mean
the coastline. Also the tides are different. I feel the Pacific is
different from the Atlantic. Not only the difference between sea
and ocean but even between two seas and two oceans. All the
natural phenomena interest me. When I was a child I wanted to
look into the sun without closing my eyes. I was very impressed
by the sun. The strong Mediterranean sun. It really enters you.
You swim and are right under it, that's very impressive.

The sun is the protagonist of The Arab Apocalypse, *one of your
most intense poetry cycles.*

It's all built on that. The power of the sun. I don't know how
children dream, but in their drawings there is very often a sun.
So the sun must be important to them. Then they get used to
it. We get used to things. But the sun is extraordinary. Just like
a sunset when the whole world becomes a festival of colors. We
have created cities and an architecture which no longer exposes
us to nature.

What was the situation when you decided to write The Arab
Apocalypse?

It was in January 1975. One day I took a pencil, a paper, and I
said to myself: I want to write a poem on the sun. Totally repet-
itive: the sun, the sun, the sun. I wrote a first page, and it stayed
inmy drawer. Then, in April 1975, the Christian militia, the
Phalanges, killed a whole Palestinian busload. They stopped
the bus and killed everybody. And I got cold, you know. I knew
this would cause big trouble in the city. Everybody was upset
about what will happen next. It was a provocation. Israeli air-
planes came. But they didn't bomb. They just turned around.
That's what I called: the night of non-event. We were waiting
for something to explode. So my poem on the sun had already
changed. As I say: History wrote that poem, not me. After the
first, the second page, I found a thing very important in art, in
writing. That's rhythm. It's like when you walk. When you find
your rhythm, you can walk a lot.

For my poem I found those long self-sufficient lines. Then the Palestinians started shooting back. After a while the war got more and more violent, bloody, and there was a camp. I speak of Tell Zaatar. Tell Zaatar means "the hill of thyme." It was on the way out of Beirut, on the road to Damascus. It was a kind of neighborhood where there were Christians, Muslims, all of them poor people. The Phalanges decided to destroy that camp. I was living in East Beirut, in a tenth-floor apartment, and from the balcony I saw the bombs falling on Tell Zaatar, I heard the explosions. I knew that under every explosion people were dying. They circled the camp. Many of the fighters had left early. But the women, the children, the old people stayed there. The siege of Tell Zaatar took fifty-nine days. So I wrote fifty-nine chapters for the fifty-nine days of the siege of Tell Zaatar. It was the beginning of lots of bad mistakes. It was an Apocalypse, not only for Lebanon but the whole Arab World. That's the essence of my book. We started a tornado, a culture of blind violence. We didn't think it will last fifteen years. They didn't think what will happen after. We'll destroy and tomorrow we'll see. I saw how people changed. Young men who were friends of mine, overnight became killers. This is civil war. Whatever you shoot, you shoot your own. It is sheer madness.

Your poetry expresses desperation and anger, but also love.

Yes, it's awful. I love those countries. Egypt, Yemen, Iraq. The Americans destroyed Iraq, but Saddam made it easy for them. Look at Syria. All these countries are in a vortex. This is what I call an Apocalypse. If it had been all about Lebanon, I would have written something else. What hurts me so much is that it is a cosmic phenomenon. The enemy. The strangers. That's our country. Away with them. The same kind of language everywhere.

In thinking about poetry, painting, philosophy let's also think about language. What would you define as your "language"?

Well, you see, I have been an unwilling pioneer in many things. I was one of the first women in Beirut who went to work at age sixteen, seventeen. Women were not allowed then to work. I was maybe one of the few who left home at twenty-four and went all the way to California alone, with no money and not knowing what I was doing and where I was going. Today everyone is on a plane, everyone's in a way global. With language it's the same. Fifty years ago, in Paris you heard only French. Now you hear lots of languages, Italian and Spanish most of all. The Russians started to buy houses, the Chinese are buying apartments, not only in Paris but in France. So languages are more and more being mixed. In my generation I was a bit special. But only because our cultures were closed in themselves. In the Middle Ages people already wrote in different languages. For example, Dante wrote in Latin and he wrote in Italian. The Sufis, some of them like Rumi, wrote in Arabic, Turkish, and Persian. Not letters. Poetry.

My language should have been Arabic, but I went to French schools and was forbidden to speak Arabic. A type of cultural genocide. Maybe I should not use such a strict expression, but that's the way it was. Preventing people from speaking their

own language is colonialism. At home we didn't speak Arabic
either because my mother was Greek. A Greek from Smyrna.
My father was an Arab, but an Ottoman officer, he spoke Turk-
ish with my mother. So I grew up speaking Greek, she spoke
only Greek with me and Turkish with my father. What is my
maternal language? Well, not the language I write in. I went to
French schools. I speak Turkish, Arabic, and Greek but I don't
write these languages. I have forgotten a lot about Turkish, but
Greek I can do quite well. I have been often in Greece. When
I came to the United States I learned English, which became
very natural to me. So I write in two languages which are not
my family's languages, but I think the world is going in that
direction. Not to write in one's native language is becoming
common.

When writing about you, there is always an attempt to classify
you. Some call you an Arab poet. Others say: She is American.
Or: No, she belongs more to the Greek world. That means, to
Europe. Besides, she has lived for a long time in Paris. Still
others: Forget about it, let's call her a cosmopolitan.

Maybe I am really American now, not only because I have an
American passport. I lived fifty years in America and I think in
American. This is not necessarily so. You can live somewhere
for fifty years and not become part of that place. And why
not? There are Arab immigrants from Algeria, and in Paris they
are Algerians. Well, leave them alone. They will die one day,
their children are becoming French because they go to French
schools. So where's the problem. We want to fight, and we use

everything for a fight. What does it bother me if my neigh-
bor doesn't want to speak French in Paris? It's his problem. It's
his choice, you see. We have to open up to diversity. I am an
Arab poet and I am an American poet and sometimes I write in
French. Why not. If you had four children, you would love all
four, you would not break your heart into four pieces. You love
each one totally. For example, you can be completely Turkish
and all German or all American, you are always yourself.

*Then, in the globalized world, we should re-pose the question
of identity.*

Identity can be multiple. You yourself have a son, he's Italian
and he is German. Why should he choose one or the other? It
is difficult only when one of the sides to which one belongs, is
at war. Then I would say that you should choose justice, that
which seems just to you. For example, if you are both Palestin-
ian and Jewish, how can you live with it? Either one chooses
one side and gets torn in half. Or one says: I am both, I have to
deal with it. Everyone has to decide for themselves.

*Certainly one should choose the side of justice, but also that of
love. Justice and love are intrinsically connected I would say.
In your essay,* The Cost for Love We Are Not Willing to Pay, *
written for dOCUMENTA (13), you wrote about love as "the
only salvation" possible.*

Love … what is love? As soon as you try to define something,
it escapes you. What is bread? You eat it. You say: what is a

flower? What is the world? We are in the world. When you think too much, in the beginning you think you are grasping reality and then it escapes you. Love is something we feel. It's an attraction, a spell that emanates from something that becomes more important than yourself, but at the same time gives you meaning. Positive love, there are all kinds of love, you can feel also negative love. Love, positive love, opens something in you without which you cannot live. And if you lose that, you feel impoverished. You feel something important is missing. You love a person, when this person is there you are different, you are happier, you are richer in yourself. You look at the sky and find it more beautiful than the day before. Love enlightens you, it is an epiphany, an ecstatic feeling. And when that object of love is removed you feel pain. You miss it and you feel your life is meaningless. But you can also love poetry, you can love paintings. But the most extraordinary, the most perfect love is to love another person. Because this other person speaks back to you. You may love a poem, but the poet is not there. You love a painting, but suddenly you are alone. The love disappears and you are in front of an object.

What of love in relation to a certain mountain, Mount Tamalpais?

I loved this mountain. Maybe because I was so destroyed, I had lost someone I loved, and I didn't want to love a human being anymore. I was happy in a normal way, going to concerts, reading books, but I felt alone in California and the mountain that I saw from my window became a pole, an axis around which

I moved, a center. It became my point of reference. When I saw it from afar, I became peaceful. Like something safe in your life, you are in the middle of an ocean and suddenly there is a light or a star in the sky that speaks to you … really, this happens. Since I'm a painter, I painted the mountain. So I had a big dialogue with it, and it spoke to me because it changed all the time. Things do speak. When I said: You are standing in front of a painting, I said: The painting speaks to you. But it may fall silent. Suddenly you are indifferent or you're tired, you go to another painting. The mountain does not go away, it is there, it has always been there. I started watching it. For forty years it was never the same for a single second.

You wrote a beautiful book about this mountain, your Journey to Mount Tamalpais. *You've been circling the mountain again and again, in reality and in your dreams, and also in poetry. You drew and painted it countless times. The longer I thought about this mountain and your relationship with it, the more it seemed to me as a connection to something divine. Are you a religious person?*

No, not really, but it depends on what we mean by religion. I respect religion. I think people are entitled to their religion. If they want to be Muslim or Jewish or Christian. I would never stop or criticize them or their religion. Of course, they may also misuse the religion, that's a personal thing, not the religion as a whole. Religions are also open to criticism, religions in themselves are not perfect. There are very violent things in the Bible and in the Koran, less so in the Gospels. Christians have done much violence, but the Gospels are not really violent. I am not religious in the sense that I perform the rites of any religion. I didn't choose a religion. My father was Muslim, my mother was Christian. I understand both, I like both religions but I couldn't decide: Am I a Muslim or am I a Christian? I'm not a person who follows rules and goes to church or prayers five times a day. But I have a sense of what religion sometimes speaks about: the beyondness.

That beyondness I call the universe, and I think people call it God, and maybe, maybe there really is something that some religious people think of when they speak of God. I don't know what they mean by that, but I don't know what I mean by "universe" either. It's there. All I know is that our mind, as strong as it is, doesn't know everything and that there are worlds that it doesn't know, not only things in this world, but literally other worlds we don't know. I'm sensitive not to close things. I am not a positivist, no. What is mystical in spirits, in souls? I don't know, maybe poetry is, or painting, or music, sometimes meditation in silence. I'm amazed at the possibilities of the mind and also of the potentialities that the mind cannot reach. We are living mystery. Poetry and the arts try to catch it. Not the mystery itself, but its sense, its meaning. To open up somebody else's mind to that mystery, as Cézanne did: He opens you to the mystery of an apple.

Apart from Cézanne or Magritte or Picasso, who mean a lot to you, are there any of the artists you admire?

Of course I have friends who are really good painters. For exam-
ple, a friend in Montana, Russell Chatham, he's a great painter.
He paints wonderful landscapes. My friend Simone Fattal is a
brilliant sculptor. Eugénie Paultre is an amazing painter. With
every shade a great person may be born. Everybody counts, not
even the well-known so-called great personalities. I like artists
who think freely, like Gerhard Richter, for example. Or artists
who were or are engaged with their time, like Anselm Kiefer or
Heiner Müller. My poetry is also concerned with what is going
on. I like artists who are political, like Brandon Shimoda. We
need them. Constantly. The destructive people are so strong
that we have to react to them permanently, we need to create an
answer to that. Artists can do that. They are free enough to do
what they want. Or they should be. That's my personal wish. I
like the writers and the poets who are aware of the world as it
is. Of course, they are not forced to take care of the world, but
I wish they did, because the world needs them.

*When we met in the late nineties, you told me: One has to
make sure to balance, to give to the positive side as much coun-
terweight as possible. This concerns artists, but it also affects
each and every one of us. These are often the supposedly small
things. For example, get up every morning, make breakfast for
the children, take them to school. To live our everyday life con-
sciously and responsibly.*

Yes, this is a big thing. I grew up with a mother who came
from a very poor family. She valued everything. She was very

religious. She did not really go to church, but she believed in the Virgin Mary, she talked to her. She said: Thank you, Virgin Mary, that I have a roof. Because she was almost on the street when she met my father. He was twenty years older than she, and he was a top officer, he had another religion. No Greek girl had married a Muslim. She did, and she always said: Thank God, he saved me. Sometimes she cleaned a pot saying: look how it shines, like the moon! She was happy that she had nice pots. And a kitchen. She has been thanking for all her life that she had a roof and food on the table. Once, when I was walking through Beirut, I saw colorfully dressed Kurdish women, sitting by the sidewalk waiting for a job, you could go and take one of them. One day I was eating oranges in the street and threw away the peel. Two of these women came and ate the peel, the peel of the orange. I never forgot it. It was overwhelming.

If you had some wishes, what would you wish for?

What I would wish for? Me? What I wish for myself is that I don't have to suffer between now and my death. I do not want to dissolve gradually, that's terrible for yourself and for all who are around you. This is a very personal wish. By the way, I wish for more great music and art. I mean, there are billions of people, so many artists, and we seldom see or hear something that really astonishes us. I'd like to see a play which I will not forget. I wish for playwrights like Brecht or Heiner Müller or composers like Mozart was for his time. Who is a great composer in life today? Lots are very good, but they are not unforgettable.

You go to fifty plays and maybe you see one that touches you. You hear who knows how many concerts and among them is perhaps one that you will not forget.

But if you happen to hear such a concert, for example, are not you happy to be alive?

Yes, you are happy you are alive and you saw that, you heard that. It enriches you. I wish for people, myself included, to see more of nature before we spoil the great wilderness. I wish more peace, also for the Arab world. It's in turmoil. It's a shame that it happened. People just got used to it.

Do you think it is possible for people to be moved, to stop getting used to such things?

Who knows. I wish people would become more upset, more angry and also more innocent. We have lost a lot of innocence. People are no longer simple enough to say: How beautiful, or, how awful! Maybe this is still different in some villages, but it has disappeared.

This may be related to the changes we talked about, from nature to cities, or a form of anonymity.

When somebody died in my neighborhood when I was a child, my mother would say: Don't laugh, the neighbors may hear, you know they mourn, they lost somebody. The whole street was involved: poor guy, he lost his wife or his child. Somebody died and it was a big event in the street. I went to some funerals in the United States and felt that they did not bury the person, they got rid of him or her. You see, they finish, put it behind them, and they go to work. Not that they don't feel, but they feel it all alone, for themselves. There is no connection, no family. Or they have to work and their office doesn't give them time to cry.

What can you do about it? What else do you wish for?

Yes, I would wish for more solidarity. We think that we have wealth, but we also have a lot of poor people and a lot of fear. We have lost solidarity among the poor. My family was never poor but my mother was haunted by poverty. We were not rich either, and she was always aware that there is real poverty. Once she met a Greek woman, a Catholic Greek, a stranger in Beirut, she was sick and on the street, like a homeless person. My mother went to a Catholic church and she gave hell to the priest. She said: Why do you call yourself Christians and you have people like her that you do not care about? They gave her something like two dollars for this woman and my mother was shocked. I heard that, I saw that when I was a child. I am happy I did. Because of this I know that other people have great difficulties. For example: At night, at seven, eight in the evening, if there was food left, my mother put it in a pot and my father went and took it to the people in our street. There was always a family poorer than us and you brought food to them.

Today we throw it away. Poverty became anonymous. The Koran says you should give twenty percent of your money to charity. Nobody gives a penny today. The Muslim world is like Europe. We always talk in abstractions. As far as human solidarity is concerned, we rely on institutions. But there are countries that lost their solidarity and have no institutions. Of course some countries have social security but it becomes more and more anonymous. Then the governments want to cut into that. There's no other choice. Before you depended on the family, now you depend on the government. Europe is also in danger. Look, every door in my street in Paris is locked. It has to have codes, numbers. Suppose you are ill, you want to rest, sit somewhere, there's nowhere to sit. Before you opened a door and sat on the stairways. Maybe those are little things. But they are important. Yes, I would wish for more solidarity.

Mayakovsky

1

Mayakovsky, where are you?

I can go to the train station
and pick you up,

we can speak of the weather
on the way back,

and if you're coming by bus
I can wait for you at the
terminal

and in case you found enough
money to have taken the plane,

I will get up early and wait
for you.

Don't tell me dear Vladimir
that you lost my address,

and that you won't come,
not tomorrow, not ever,

I will still wait for you
because we're feeling miserable

here, and elsewhere, in Europe
or in California.

We all know that your
revolution was bloody

but now the world is letting blood
with no change, no hope,
in sight

You are underfoot, Mayakovsky
I mean if your bones held together,

in spite of the years,

let me inform you that
poets are leaving their rooms,
by the hundreds,

in search of you, in every
train, plane and streetcar,

and, at night, in the harbors.

2

In a fugitive and dull light
I'm listening to a ball game

staring at a point in space
between the radio and Mayakovsky

my team has not been leading
since the revolution faltered

under our expectations' dire
weight

so we pretend to play chess
with Russians

or go skiing in the Arctic
like Norwegians on a holiday
outing

but it's the problems
that are coming to us,

finding us reading your books,
Mayakovsky, their pages yellowed
with dust;
we're one hundred years younger,
waiting with you for the signal
that will change the world.

3

I keep asking where the poet
is hiding and get smiles and
looks of bewilderment for an answer

I go through the alleys of the
city, hoping to see him standing
by a window

I knocked at Lili Brik's door,
her neighbors shouted that she
had gone to Paris

I read the papers and the obituaries,
but can't find his name.

It is not dark, tonight
in Moscow, because of the snow.

Back, in the hotel, there's
this phone call: Mayakovsky has
committed suicide ...

I didn't know.

4

In the Berezina of my childhood
soldiers were freezing to death
and Napoleon was losing the war

I was crying for the horses because,
lying on their backs, they loomed
bigger than my parents.

These days, I hang around some
North Beach cafés, yearning for signs
of adventure.

Something, though, is pressing on
my breathing. Customers are happy

at this special moment, celebrating
the season,

I'm confused.

5

This moment's future is going to be too
wretched to matter. The news creates
alienation and fear.

Illumination is to be found in oak
trees, not in my heart. I'm searching
for a poet with whom to share a night
of conversation.

I remember that trains in Turkey were
producing carbon dioxide when the
empire was crumbling

and that women were drinking tea by
the edge of their desires.

6

I have friends who write mystic poems
on ecstatic days, their bare feet
playing with the ocean. Their cars
shine at their door, wagging their
tails with impatience.

Theirs are nice poems unveiling the
world the way young men uncover their
first love.

I have other friends—it's true that
they live far from the Bay—who encode
their poems on the skin of their brain.
They live in places so crowded that
they take turns and sleep two hours at
a time.

As the siege prevents them from finding
paper and ink, they dream of cutting
their veins, one morning, to write a
letter to their mother.

7

Mayakovsky, the twin brothers
Blood and Death led you into their
dark chambers, immured and empty,

but your secret visions are traveling
from country to country, lodging
in different minds, and different
buildings.

8

Collecting food for the soul in
grammar books keeps us from moving

further; we lose speech, song and
cohesion.

Should we stay where we are, with
ideas about immortality bowling like
the sun itself, yesterday, visibly
a furnace ready to reduce everything
to radiating beams.

9

Did someone run you ashore on that
oceanic night or did pantalooned
clouds drop you on the pavement
while the Army was celebrating
May Day?

I want a parade for the fallen poet,
a minute of silence, some flowers …
There, silently crying between her
son's inanimate body and yours, I
see Akhmatova.

10

There was, long before you and I
were born, a woman, with a blue
apron, pouring milk in a
painter's cup.

Then you appeared,
tall, wild and unconcerned,
on the lit stage of her
kitchen.

The years were turbulent,
students were reading you in
their beds in their seasons of
high fever

and Vermeer was working on your
portrait.

11

Mayakovsky, wherefrom the wind that
will carry my thoughts to you?

They're all gone: Imam Ali, the Che,
Ghassan Kanafani and you ...

the hard ones remain.

This spring, the planets aligned
themselves like prisoners waiting
to be mowed down ... in the splendor of
an immense sky

words stuck in my throat are
shiny pebbles,

the bullet that
killed you.

We are angry, and you know
what it means

12

Dear M,

With their shirts worn
inside out,
their dieting and
crying

—they're too rich, of course,

they go on, plundering jungles,
taming rivers and
discoursing on pleasure boats.

Some of us think that you are
not worse off
in your non-world
than the emaciated people who
crowd the barrios of the
Americas.

13

Dearest,

colors swirl within
one's brain

when one looks
into the void

left by the departure
of time

energy particles
pour into the eyes

and one ceases to
consider if it's

better to live
or to die.

The Unfolding of An Artist's Book

In the very early days of the sixties I was introduced to a person who was spending his life sitting in two or three eating places in San Francisco and drawing ceaselessly the faces of the people around, their hands, most often. The day I met him: It was at the Buena Vista Cafe, then a much frequented bar and cafe by Beach and Hyde, famous for its Irish coffee and its proximity to both the end of the cable-car line and the Playhouse Theatre.

Rick Banon should have been a San Francisco legend. But he lived in a kind of anonymity, I should say clandestinity, because he was a thorough opium smoker and lonelier than a sailor. He had gone to China in the forties and came back to the U.S. with a habit, a Chinese brass inkpot, a brush, and some Chinese scrolls in the form of folding books, accordion-like books which are also part of the Japanese tradition in art.

The inkpot fitted in the inside pocket of his jacket, a kind of a tube in which he could also install (carefully) his slim and precious brush. He was thus constantly totally equipped. He refused to be called an artist when he showed me his working materials. "I am just drawing," he said, and then he added: "I am not a painter but a writer. One day in Peking I was sitting on the main square drawing a chrysanthemum and a little boy stopped close, looked at what I was doing, and told his father: 'Look, he is writing a chrysanthemum.' He was right. I am a writer."

Rick was in fact a great intellect. In his (miserable) room on Geary by Van Ness, he would read for hours, days, and discuss his thoughts with the two or three friends he had in the city. He would eat in the dingiest places and use his meager veteran's subsidies to buy his dope, his folding books, his China inks, and the drinks he had to order in the two or three cafes in which he was spending the hours out of his room. To make things harder for himself he was an insomniac, half sleeping in the smoke of his pipes.

Before that fateful afternoon, I had never seen any folding books. He opened the one he was working on, put it on the table after having pushed his drink and dried the surface, and I was in a state of wonder: tiny heads were drawn, each with its own character, the customers of the cafe were recorded with utmost care, filling every page of the book the way they were crowding the place as well as Rick's mind. Here and there, tucked in what were empty places on the paper, were fingers holding cigarettes, swirls of smoke, an obsessed and obsessive mass of humanity running like a river all along the book, which was so to speak growing in length, like a ribbon.

Thus one of the most lasting of my artistic impressions was happening amidst a crowd in the magic atmosphere of San Francisco, which was still primarily a harbor with all the feelings of alcohol and transiency that harbors create.

At our next encounter Rick was starting a book. He had already covered a few pages when I arrived and in a short while looked at me, passed on the work to my hands and said that I surely would like to work the way he did, and that the book was mine to continue. It was clearly a mystic transfer, a gesture in the logic of being, something that came from a place preceding

him and that had to go, to keep going, to acquire a new tran-
siency, an open-ended trust.

When I came home, unfolded the book and looked at my
own brushes and inks, I thought that I had to do some draw-
ings the way I knew. I drew, I remember, a Chinese ginger vase
that I had, then a flower pot with some flowers, then my own
inkpot … so different from Rick's drawings!

But that new format started to preoccupy my mind: I had
to do something I never did, to find a way of thinking ade-
quate—for me—to this new material. I realized how much
materials, for artists, are things that mediate thought, how
much they condition one's aesthetic choices, how much
they become the elements of one's expression, and instead of
being just a support, they become in a way a co-author of
one's work.

I know I'm telling a story, but story is always superior
to theory, albeit theory is … another story. Things happen in
time; therefore they always constitute a story: the unfolding
of one's mental operations is akin, it appeared to me, to these
long horizontal scrolls that are not meant to be grasped in a
single vision like a painting, but rather could be read, visually,
in sequence, like an ordinary book that you cannot read in a
single glance.

This sense of reading attached to the very format of these
"scrolls" brought to my mind poetry and literature. I felt that
kinship between script and the horizontality of the paper. I
suddenly saw that I was going to write poetry on these papers
and paint watercolors with the sentences, verses, or words.
I opened up to myself, with exhilaration, a new artistic world

whose possibilities I was going to explore by the very acts of painting.

I used Arabic poems: Arabic script has in its essence infinite possibilities, and of course they have been explored and practically exhausted by classical calligraphy and by the geometric patterns made of sacred verses, and turned into clay tiles which ornament the great mosques of the Islamic world.

My endeavor had nothing to do directly with this classical heritage, which is based on the codification of script and on the perfection of codified brush strokes.

I used my (extremely imperfect) handwriting, figuring out the visual possibilities of the manipulation of letters and words given the elasticity of Arabic script. To give an example: a single letter can be as short as the tiniest possible script or can be extended to cover a whole page or, by extension, any size possible or imagined.

I was more than just interested in this new approach, I was having the feeling that there was something sacred about it. I felt close to the icon painters of the past: they were in awe of the fact that they were dealing with sacred history. I was dealing with the combination of poetry, script, and painting, I was finding a way out from the past (classical calligraphy), and still carrying on to new shores the inherent possibilities of Arabic writing: I was discovering, by experiencing it, that writing and drawing were one. So, the watercolors or ink drawings and the writing of the poetry were constantly unified in the visual field of the artwork.

I remember how carefully I used to wash my hands, with what care and apprehension I was choosing a particular scroll, with what interest I was looking at the paper, usually Japanese handmade paper or rice paper made in Kyoto, because everything had to be in tune: the size, the format, the text, the colors, the texture of these colors, the light outside, my own availability. It was each time like entering into a religion for a believer, like going for a climb for an alpinist, as if painting in this case was also a sacred sport, a battle both spiritual and physical, as well as a game of chance.

When one starts a work which can be as long, when unfolded, as 200 inches or 400 inches … one knows that no mistakes are allowed, that the rhythm has to be kept as long as working endures, that this is a trip, a travel, an adventure, something that awakens in the depth of the species memory images, or memories of the nomadic essence of the spirit. In the meantime, the very presence of size and format, which is part of the experience of a painting (framed or not), seems to disappear with these books when stretched out, and the modular character of the work transpires and enchants, exactly as is the case with music.

Thus, the usual affinity between painting and literature, in representational art, and between painting and philosophy, in abstract or conceptual art, gives way to the presence of an affinity between painting, or the visual arts, and music. The response to the interplay of themes and variations, so essential to music, the awareness of pure compositional values, become here major concerns of both music and the folded painted book, which by the way, in multiplying the possibilities of combinations of different "pages," opens up for music itself infinite temptations of modular combinations and recurrences.

Asked, if the drawings and watercolors which I mingle with the written texts are "illustrations," I have to answer that they are not; they are, rather, an "equivalence," both a response and a counterpoint to the text used, not only on a visual structural basis but also as a means to convey a reading, an intellectual and emotional response to the poetry. Instead of explaining, analyzing my understanding of a particular poem or text in word-language, I utilize the language of painting: in this case, written words and the visual text mirror each other and form a new entity which combines them both.

Working for years (since about 1963) in this manner, first exclusively with Arabic texts and then also with some works from American or French poets, I discovered a new dimension to the notion of translation. Translation is transportation. One carries, let's say, a poem or a text in prose, from one language into another, from one language-universe, into another. This operation implies many questions, some of which are metaphysical, such as: Do two readers really read the same text when they do? Who's the "author" of the translated text? What is the real being of the original text and the one of the second?

A shower of questions manifested themselves in the course of these many year-long experiences. These "artist's books" were meant to show how one sensibility reacted, responded to the one of the poetic text inscribed; how one's understanding of the poetic text was carried from one language to another, this latter being visual; how the finished work in some ways becomes independent from both the written element and the image, by being seen as forming a new entity which is itself then created by the viewers, their vision differing from person to person ad infinitum.

To put it succinctly: this approach, which combines liter-
ature and art, and which has been fundamental to Chinese
and Japanese art, and which is transformed here, seems
to bring out a sense of becoming, of fluidity, of constant
transformation, as being essential to the mind: the mind
never rests on these scrolls as it moves back and forth on them
as a scanner. This experience transforms these visual, written
words, and the paintings of which they are a part, into a kind
of musical score that each person, including their maker,
translates into his/her inner languages, into that which we call
the understanding.

Working for years in this direction led me to the suspicion
that our mental world is an ongoing "translation," that per-
ception is a translating of the object of that perception, and
that any thought that we may think to be primary, primor-
dial, spontaneous, is already an interpretation of something
which precedes it and may even be of another nature, another
"stuff" than thinking itself, a wavelength, an "it" which remains
unknown, a translation of this "it" by an active filtering func-
tion we call the "mind."

On a practical level, all these reflections gradually led me to
the erasure, once in a while, of the written text, keeping very
little of it or none at all, and made me paint on these "books"
unfolding landscapes or abstract paintings, not as a return to
realistic or abstract art, but to a vision of reality as a permanently
transformed score meant to remain obscure as such but "heard"
or "seen" through the translatorial powers of our minds. Thus,
although a painted landscape on a traditional canvas freezes, so
to speak, its subject matter, a landscape on these accordion-like

books can be seen in different manners, the first two openings juxtaposed, for example, with later ones, at will, so that a single landscape becomes many, according to the way the work is folded. We move away from the fixed image and see combinations of the same reality, the birth of different realities out of a single one. To put it simply: by multiplying the elements of a work which is itself open-ended, one calls for an intense participation of the mind, for the collaboration of its various powers, and this process illuminates, brings into presence multiple presences, and it is no coincidence that, historically, the traditional and ancient works combining words and images were called by the magic name of Illuminations.

The Cost for Love
We Are Not Willing to Pay

This text was written for the booklet accompanying the exhibition of the artist's work at dOCUMENTA (13), in Kassel, Germany, 2012.

In the last weeks preceding the collapse of his rational powers, Nietzsche wrote, "I am a rendez-vous of experiences"; the word is indeed *rendez-vous*. He meant that he had spent his life running toward the world and that the world had been running toward him. This double attraction, this movement, had been central. The immense generosity of his mind had made him the meeting point of cosmic forces, of the social currents of his time, and of the ideas that he seemed so often more to capture than to create. This generosity was a form of love. He showed us in a radical way not the love solely of Being but also of more apparently menial things, of everything that touched his mind—and his heart. That is why there's no system, no hard center to his work, but a series of fundamental intuitions.

Strangely enough, Nietzsche brings to my mind the memory of al-Hallaj, though the (Islamic) mysticism of the latter can appear to be at the opposite end of Nietzsche's views.

The German philosopher and the tenth-century Arab mystic pushed their creative energies as far as possible, self-sacrificing for their radical commitments. Al-Hallaj had said: "I am the creative Truth." He affirmed: "I have seen my Lord with the heart's eye, and asked Him, 'Who are You?' He answered to me: 'You!'"

And in his *Dithyrambs of Dionysus*, Nietzsche indirectly refers to himself as a man who declared, "I am the Truth." Thus both let themselves be consumed by an itinerary toward the absolute: God, for the one, the transmutation (and explosion) of values, for the other. The overriding principle that ruled al-Hallaj was love, the desire to approach and penetrate the fire of the divine will until death. Al-Hallaj welcomed his condemnation to death by torture and crucifixion as a natural price for his passion. As for himself, Nietzsche chose, as a price for the freedom to pursue his search, an utter solitude that led him to insanity.

Nietzsche's intense commitment to his revolutionary and revelatory thinking was doubled by his love for Cosima: In the last writings of his mentally troubled years, he expressed hatred for practically everyone he had ever known, save Cosima Wagner, and his last conscious utterance seems to have been a note he sent her in which he declared (desperately, to say the least): "Ariadne, I love you, Dionysus!"

It is difficult to dismiss the overwhelming love that fuels the energy of the mystics from all religions. Even non-believers can marvel, for example, at the writings of the great Sufi masters, where poetry, philosophical questionings, and profound lyricism fuse around the intense human desire to reach the divine.

More than any other field of expression, mystical texts witness the experience of the fundamental unity of love. By that it is meant that although we differentiate the diverse expressions of love, we feel that they all come from a single source: like electric energy that branches out into different (and contradictory) manifestations, love applies itself to Nature, to sexual impulse, to family ties, to science, and so on ... it proceeds from a single core hidden in the brain and its ancestry, as well as in the mysterious realms of what we call the "outside world."

Although popular belief holds love in its most common use as romance or passion, it does not need to be that reductive. I can recall in my own existence two passions that did not concern human beings but that at turns took center stage.

Growing up in Beirut in the 1930s, I was one of a handful of children taken to the sea to swim. The city didn't yet have the oceanside resorts that people enjoy nowadays in the summer. The sea beat directly against the edges of the town, and there were rocks with little pools just half a mile from my house. My mother would sit on one of these rocks and let me paddle in the water. As a measure of security, she passed under my arms a string or a cord, something like a leash that she held carefully. Thus I developed from my early years a sensuous response to the sea, a fascination, a need that I lived like a secret. It enchanted me, and it isolated me. It has lasted all my life.

A few decades later, I settled in California. During the first years there, I carried with me the feeling of a deep uprootedness. Living north of San Francisco, near the other side of the Golden Gate Bridge, I developed a familiarity with Mount Tamalpais, a mountain that dominates the scene. Gradually, the mountain became a reference point. I began to orient myself by its presence, or a view of it in the distance. It became a companion. As, at a certain time, I became a painter, I started to make drawings of it, oils. I moved to Sausalito, living in a house whose windows were filled by its view. I painted nothing else but this for years, until I couldn't think of anything else. To observe its constant changes became my major preoccupation.

I even wrote a book in order to come to terms with it—but the experience overflowed my writing. I was addicted.

Yes, I used to go to the little jazz joints, visit the ocean, drive to Yosemite Valley, breathe fully California's weather ... but that was all. I had forgotten the possibility of any other kind of private life! I don't regret it. On the contrary, those were ecstatic years.

Some would say that love for a particular tree, or even for Nature, is benign; but no love is benign. It can and does engage one's whole being. What we call "Nature" covers an infinite number of responses. It involves exploration, risk taking, revolution in one's life. It can take you to the top of the Himalayas, to a ridge of volcanoes, to caves or laboratories; it will reveal your self to yourself; it will inspire artists, poets, and philosophers; it will open ways to the understanding of grandeur.

More and more people behave as if they ignore Nature, dislike it, or even despise it. We wouldn't have the ecological catastrophe in which we live if it were otherwise. They absolutely cannot understand Native American Chief Joseph's response to American settlers when they tried to use Indians to plow the land: "How can I split my mother's belly with a plough?"—and he meant it not metaphorically, but literally. After all, Earth is mother. It sustains life. We come from it: religious say it in their way, science says it too, as well as common sense. So we do not love our first, our original, mother. We quit her. We left her behind. We went to the moon.

On the symbolic level, it's absolutely true that we lost interest in our nomadic planet. The most advanced research in the world nowadays concerns either the infinitely small (the field of the atom) or astronomy. Mankind is already exploring the sustainability of life on other planets ... technology is totally at the service of abstract science and its involvement with non-imaginable matters. Planet Earth is old news. It's the house we are discarding. We definitely don't love her. We almost believe we don't need her. Because the price for the love that will save her would reach an almost impossible level. It would require that we change radically our ways of life, that we give up many of our comforts, our toys, our gadgets, and above all our political and religious mythologies. We would have to create a new world (not a Brave New World!). We're not ready to do all that. So we are, very simply, doomed.

We can also evoke all the political militants, the heroes of liberation movements, the real fighters for human rights, the rebels ... and what do we do with them? We make them end in mental hospitals, in prisons, in exile ... only the lovers of power, money, war, and organized crime seem to move in full light. We are in a moment of history when Western democracies that thought of themselves as the cutting edge of freedom are seeing their values eroding, their freedoms put into question, their humanism getting lost, all this because their awareness that their power is diminishing on the world scene is creating in them sheer panic. What must be done? Most urgently, we ought to find the sense of human solidarity without which no society is coherent. On November 5, 1873, Tolstoy wrote in his diary: "Love is disturbing." Yes, political activism is a way of love, and it's explosive, and it can lead to great upheavals. But what if we do not take those risks, what if we're deter-mined to maintain the present state of affairs, playing it (only apparently) safe? The answer is simple: By not paying the price for what it takes to change the world, the world will change in its own way, will change anyway, will escape the possibility we possess to direct it along roads we deem beneficial, and the price will end up being much higher, and it will be too late! The problem—to make things worse—is universal.

And now, we may muse on love in its most overused incarnation, the way people have used it since time immemorial, although it is today the most misunderstood, and the most commercialized, of all its forms.

But love in its most genuine meaning exists. It can start in childhood: by the age of nine, ten, children start having an infatuation with one of their classmates, another child who arrests their attention—and their heart. They already sense the difference between friendship and love.

Love begins with the awareness of the curve of the back, the length of an eyebrow, the beginning of a smile. "It happens!" The presence of another being mobilizes your attention, your senses. That feeling grows, becomes a desire to repeat the experience. It becomes an itinerary. A voyage. The imagination takes over that reality and starts building fantasies, dreams, projects … It creates its own necessity, and in some people encompasses the whole of life. It becomes that voice in the night that tells you "I love you," and that knocks your whole being off balance. Ultimately, it reaches the zones where you question the whole universe; it domesticates thinking, it ends as an addiction. And then, in the tragic cases, it falls into an abyss, where there are cries of pain, where the lovers lose sense of all dimensions, of all reality. These are times when a poet can say that love changes the direction of time.

This state of being in love is an uneasy state: it is unstable, permeable to all winds, almost irrational. It easily creates a sense of terror, becomes obsessive. That's when heartbeats accelerate, and one puts out the lights, lies down with another body, and sinks into a kind of desperate bliss.

How can one bear such an intensity? Love becomes a river of fire that replaces blood in the arteries. It leaves one breathless. One wants to stay still, not moving, having forgotten the hour. Even the sense of one's body disappears. The body disappears from memory. There's an immobility due to the total mobilization of the senses functioning henceforth in an altered state. Desire itself is eventually overcome. Strangely enough, this state approximates the experience of death.

Who can endure for a long time such an internal upheaval? The lovers themselves end up fearing their happiness and feel ready to destroy it. And society itself suspects such love and represses it with all its might. It considers it to be a potential subversive revolution.

Love always acts like an earthquake. It strongly affects not only lovers but also those who watch it happen. The latter become envious. A deep jealousy takes hold of them. It's no wonder that "crimes of honor" exist, and other murderous acts against women in relation to love and sexuality. The Catholic Church itself is unequivocally against the principle of pleasure in the private lives of its followers, linking sexuality only to procreation, and the emphasis on the virginity of Mary is just one example among many. There's no escape. Love has a price (like any other human expression). We are a social species, and society will always weigh on our lives.

It is true that we have reached the point where sexuality has been separated from love. Those still naive, and scared of passionate affairs that may overtake life and create misery, love movie stars or literary figures ... with more ease than they will love a partner—that is, when they do not spend their evenings reading sports magazines and watching football games. So much is spent on passions that do not demand one's direct implication ... "modern life" offers many ways to get lost in a meaningless world.

This is considered to be the liberation of the body, the body that's becoming autonomous and is recovering its rights. Sexuality as a game is given as the height of sophistication, and it is true that a grain of cynicism doesn't hurt. But a denial of emotions in the long run can and does favor violence ... Hasn't the movie industry become a world in which the imagination is unbridled only to produce either science fiction tales or stories of crime ... and hasn't pornography become a multinational industry?

But what is love? And what are we giving up when we relinquish it?

Love is not to be described, it is to be lived. We may deny it, but we know it when it takes hold of us. When something in ourselves submits the self to itself. Prisoner of oneself, that's the lover. A strange fever. It may also sometimes happen that the element that provokes love is not necessarily human. A special case. Yes.

I came to Paris from Beirut to be a student of philosophy. Like many girls, I had had many boyfriends ... For that generation, a boyfriend was somebody to walk endlessly with in the streets, to go dancing with, to talk of love with ... we had no sexual lives, but some vaguely sexual "affairs," what I would call "atmospheric" experiences, a well-being, a kind of a pride in attracting many boys, and something more, for sure, a stirring in the body, a desire not named desire … and we thought that we were quite sophisticated, as we were the very first generation of girls allowed to have some (limited) access to young men. It was considered a great adventure!

When I first lived in Paris, I didn't have close friends. Understandingly. It took time then for foreign students to make enduring contacts with their fellow students. I felt pretty alone; but discovering the city was itself an all-consuming occupation: I was caught by it, I was happy.

I loved the night, then, as I still do. Night is an element of love; like fog. It liberates space, lets freshness cross it. Its magic elevates the body, brings to the surface the mystery of just being alive, being. With or without stars and galaxies, the sky becomes a private territory—the imagination's own scope. These are moments when one reaches all there is between the moon and oneself.

Then, on one of those cool and luminous days, those sub-dued and silvery, etching-like afternoons, I went to the Louvre Museum.

I entered that temple softly, innocently; for the first time. After a few steps, I stopped in front of *The Victory of Samothrace*. The Winged Victory. I stayed there, standing, flabbergasted. The figure was soaring, like an airplane in a silent dream. More than an airplane. A civilization was in front of my eyes taking off and still remaining on Earth, a civilization from which everything was erased save its archetypal manifestation.

And then I turned and saw the *Venus de Milo*. The statue of white marble was standing there, rising or bending according to one's place, seemingly larger than life. How long did I stand there, looking at her? Time, certainly, didn't matter. I was alone. We were alone. My eyes went over her body, which is between flesh and stone—stopped here and there, discovered her curves destined to both attract and keep at a distance, wondered at the mystery of such a presence, alive and still made of marble, meant to be not touched but dreamed about. The love that possessed the Greek sculptor in bringing this goddess to form, to shape, to life, moved over to me. All my senses awoke simultaneously. I lost my mind over her glacial yet dangerous beauty. It became an initiation. An opening into my own being. I spent this night of revelation with "her" in the most profound and meaningful solitude I have ever experienced. It was wintertime, but I spent the night perspiring. I closed my eyes and pressed my face in the pillow. I was burning with passion. I was crying. My body was demanding her presence. I was making love all by myself, and my imagination was burning.

Of course, the experiences that followed were different ... I was thrown into what people call the "real world," with everything that these words entail. But that primordial experience remained as a question, a recurring image, an epiphany: the power of art implied in that "event" remains ominous. Recollecting what had happened that night became a meditation on the nature of love ... all it did was deepen its mystery.

Before committing suicide, Mayakovsky left his succinct note: "Lili, love me!" Forgotten were the Revolution and the poetry. The impossible love (the life that failed) stared at him with an undiminished fervor.

It is true that love becomes life and to lose the one makes the other meaningless. But as most people do not dare accept the consequences of their passions, they mythologize those who live them fully, at any price, be they historical figures or romantic creations. Don't we love Anna Karenina, and read her story with real tears? Don't we see with the imagination's eye the train under which she threw her body? Don't we think secretly that she was right when we read about her in a well-heated home after the children are safely in bed? This goes for poets, too: We read and read again the story of Majnun, wandering in the Arabian desert because he won't be with Layla anymore, wandering to exhaustion; or we regret, for Rimbaud's sake, Verlaine's pitiful cowardice, Verlaine who, in his last letter, wrote to his desperate lover, of mother, wife, and church!

When in love, one becomes a bird: one stretches one's neck and hears a song not meant to be pronounced. One is speechless. But they are more and more numerous those who won't risk their lives for that moment. They won't risk even less, they won't budge. They are scared, they feel better off in their mediocrity. We can understand them: love in all its forms is the most important matter that we will ever face, but also the most dangerous, the most unpredictable, the most maddening. But it is also the only salvation I know of.

La Commedia dell'arte dei calami IV, 2015. Hand-colored etching

Untitled (Drawing Book #1), No. 7, 1990. Crayon, watercolor and pencil on paper

The Four Seasons 4, 2017. Oil on canvas

Le poids du monde III, 2016. Etching

Le poids du monde IV, 2016. Etching

Traveler, 2016. Tapestry, wool, hand-woven

California, 1977. Tapestry, wool, hand-woven

Untitled, 2010. Oil on canvas

7/35

Vue sur la mer, 2017. Etching

77

Untitled (Drawing Book #1), No. 2, 1990. Crayon, watercolor and pencil on paper

Untitled (Drawing Book #1), No. 8, 1990. Crayon, watercolor and pencil on paper

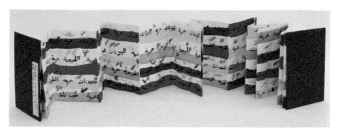

Freedom of People, Freedom of Animals, Freedom of Plants, Freedom of Nature,
2011. Leporello. Ink, watercolor and oil pastels on paper

East River Pollution "From Laura's window," *New York*, 1979. Leporello.
Crayon, pencil on Japanese paper

Installation view of the exhibit *Etel Adnan*, 2018. Zentrum Paul Klee

79

1/35   E———Adnan 17

Soleil lointain, 2017. Etching

The Adnan Songbook

British composer Gavin Bryars set a selection of eight "love poems" of Etel Adnan for the *Songbook*, first performed in 1996. They had collaborated earlier on the French section of the Robert Wilson multilingual and multicountry opera epic, *the CIVIL warS*. One of its arias, "Queen of the Sea," which appears elsewhere in this volume, became part of the Bryars cantata *Effarene*. Continuing their work together, Adnan read from her long poem *Five Senses for One Death*, with music played by the composer, at London's Serpentine Gallery in 2015.

I.

I had a gypsy
with Indian silver
all over her body
She had a
navel like the morning star
and eyes
like the meadows
of the sierras
She was a deer
and a trail
leading to an archetypal
lake

One day the sun shone
on her hair
and the forest caught fire
only the car broke down
by the curve of
the road
And we slept on a hospital bed
to rise again
like the Indian Rainbow.

II.

The sun came in
The pain went out
a window on the lone mountain
I
became
a tree decrucified
rendered
to
its roots.
2000 years of suffering redeemed
in a woman's two-days'
flight
from paradise to paradise
we went with no mule
nor train
but with our hands and our eyes.

III.

I went to the drugstore
to sell my pain
I got a penny and bought an Indian rug
on the grey wool
I read the footstep of
a sheep
on the black line   I followed a
trail
and we arrived at a meadow
there, only water talked
to us
we spoke of rain and fire
and the three of us
slept together
because we became the morning dew.

IV.

No one asked you to be an angel of
fear
or even of death
We only wanted your skin to be
as smooth
as the sea
an October afternoon
in Beirut, Lebanon
between two civil wars.
You came
with a handful of pain

and a smile
which broke the ground under my feet
as the earthquake does
when two people
meet.

V.

You are a white cloud
coming down my spine
fire moves its fingers along
my pain
but two black eyes remain
resolved in tears
and
the cloud becomes a song
I heard in the fog
and over the city
while you were counting
the money
for yesterday's hospital
bed.
We are not playing a game
of sorrow
we are trying to grow
wings
and
fly.

VI.

You are under my hands
a piece of fire
which doesn't burn itself out,
ever
You cry with the rain
and laugh every morning
at the advent of the sun
I see you
with your cousins the deer
chase shadows
under the oak trees of the ranch
You refused a
voyage to the moon
in order to
stay
a moment more
in bed.

VII.

White as the unfolded tree
of a winter in
advance
on the sun's decisions
you draw my naked body
on the city's
invisible walls
and a million tiny roads
go to a single point.

White as Ophelia's pallor
you make haggard statements
so that
madness and reason be reconciled
for ever
and the warmth of your
passion
takes on
the color of frost
white as a permanent spring.

VIII.

My hand on your hand
both
in the hollow of
a tree
one sky chasing another
sky
both
devouring atoms
and
going to the moon.
Green is the color of
space.
Two lips tasting mushrooms
and the Colorado River
haunting
the village ...
from the persistent Mediterranean

to the persistent
Pacific
we cut roads with our feet
share baggage and
food
running always one second
ahead of the running of
Time
we are travelling at some
infinite speed
we are not scared.

A Revolution Named Pina Bausch

When I received the news of her death I saw the sky darken as it did some decades ago when on the front page of a newspaper I read that the Che had been assassinated. These two beings, each in his or her own way, had revolutionized my life.

Pina Bausch opened the doors of perception by using dance, the most magical of the arts, the most primitive while also the most sophisticated of all the arts.

Raised in the era that is known as post-war, in an early childhood dominated by bombings and destruction, all her life she carried her fears, her melancholy, and her pessimism, and also in her creations.

She created a new art form, dance-theatre, neither one nor the other, but both. She threw in the air all the stuff of classical ballet: her women wore exaggerated makeup and high heels, in a parody of femininity, and her men dressed like young men, youth you can meet in the streets, who moved like adolescents inhabited by fever. They danced like young gangsters fighting, they lounged like Italians at night in Naples looking at girls and making love mentally, expending their energies in useless movements that were an enchantment to watch. She used older men to torment women, pinch them, abuse them, harass them, and lift them up like trophies, then throwing them on the ground like soiled towels … in an atmosphere of constant terror. We were always captivated because that was our own lives, intensified, scrutinized, validated by the attention they incited onstage, validated by the transmutation of terror mixed with unexpected beauty, in art.

She was compared to Brecht, at times, linked to the teachings of her dance professors and predecessors, but in fact she was unique. If I had to associate her with another figure in my mind, it would be Fassbinder: they both looked at their moment in History with utmost honesty, and more so, with total courage, and they spoke to us through the material of their choice; movement, for her, and another movement for him, that of cinema. But she resisted the suicidal instinct, creating a world more complex than the filmmaker's, a world for which music and extravagant settings generated a counterpoint, making us live an enthralling experience.

She was the more inventive in her art, the one breaking boundaries. Her choreography was often ritualistic, especially in her earlier works, showing, for example, a procession of men pursuing women like tribal dancers in a Moroccan village ... and this sense of ritual transformed the dance into a special kind of theatre. It was as if the tribal innocence was transferred to the West, and altered, and she knew all that the journey signified.

She knew that the world is still vast in its variety, and that there still remain treasures in folk or popular arts ... such as the tango, the fado, Japanese or Turkish or Indian music. She gave rigorous attention to the simple powers and enchantments that these traditions carry in themselves and that constantly renewed her imagination. And so we were, at the same time, in a cabaret and in the temple of contemporary art; at the same time, in the street and inside a theatre space, rooted in the familiar and transported far beyond.

She was a dancer and her body knew how to speak. She seems to have always proceeded from an infallible instinct. She made dance like no one before her: we were accustomed to paying attention to the dancers' legs, attitudes, curves, bends, and leaps. She used the entire body, enhancing each part: the arms, the hands, the shoulders. She had long arms, expressive hands. She danced sometimes as if she were swimming. Her arms seemed to complete the body, and she stretched them upwards, becoming a fish in water, a shark, a desperate whale. Her hands had a life of their own. They were long, expressive, flapping like birds' wings seeking the air. She was able to stand still, with her arms seducing us while they were rising up as in ancient invocations made silent. It was as if the whole body was relying on these arms, putting all its weight against them, uplifted, freed by them from gravity.

She was a force of theatre, whose genius destabilized professionals such as Heiner Müller. To the excessive character of contemporary history she responded with her excess of talent, her ability to create parallel worlds with other tools than armies and airplanes. Her performances took us into the very heart of horror, but also revived the will to survive, and for her, to survive had the colors of sunsets, the beauty of young men, and the barbaric rhythm of savage life. Her version of *The Rite of Spring* takes place in an Africa of the imagination, where the forces of the unconscious are unleashed to allow the presence of death to fuse with the origin of life.

The world of Pina Bausch: Is it theatre or dance? It is theatre because she addresses the whole range of human emotions, and it is dance because her world arises from nowhere and leads to nothing. It is a new artistic form, and very probably inimitable.

I think that one of the characters most active on her stage is Death. Everything turns around that never named entity. Her world originates in obscurity and often, especially toward the end, seeks light. The Dionysian aspect is hyperactive, ecstatic, it surges from the dark side of the moon. Her first and most intimate collaborator, Rolf Borzik, stated it clearly: "We are in the process of saying something that is already dead, or in the process of dying."

This is why desire—with its immediacy, intimacy, enhanced by dance—occupies such an important place in the vision of Pina Bausch: a desire expressed by a rough sexuality, violence, and despair. Dance is the most natural, the most suitable expression, of desire. It is desire in movement.

It starts with the courtship that mammals and birds perform to entice the females, it turns into the elegance of horsemen and the audacity of the Formula One racecar drivers. Pina's own need to seduce, her instinctive knowledge of the ways of seduction, transforms her dance-theatre into performances of eroticism.

Even the fragmentation of any action onstage is part of the strategy of desire for it to remain active, it has to be constantly interrupted, altered, shifted ... And we are also carried away by the changes of music, of gestures, of atmosphere. That instability pervades her work as in our own world. It is haunted by all kinds of instability that surround us.

With Balanchine, for example, we felt that the dance progressed by erasing its own traces, so that the memory of his pieces is that of line, light, and geometry. With Pina Bausch we remember volumes, spheres, a semi-obscurity, of music added and removed, not of movements so much as personal ways of moving. We remember a universe she denounces, and another one she reconstructs, of a precarious brutality and of beauty, also precarious.

She created instability by orchestrating her creations like musical symphonies. Profoundly romantic, she still keeps her romanticism under strict control. She withholds all possibility of coherent narration, or total crisis. By constantly breaking her rhythms, she creates an arrangement of movements that is added to other movements onstage. In fact, there's more than rhythm to her works: there's a pulse, like the beating of the heart. An essential, initial, unavoidable pulse.

When the intention is brutal, the music is romantic. When the lighting and the gestures are cruel, the music is popular, nostalgic, humane. And then, when the action onstage slows down and the situation is as trivial as possible, the music turns mechanical, electronic, obsessive; but each time we are roused, surpassing our capacities for judgment, in ecstasy.

She works in the manner of the composer Sofia Gubaidulina: fragments of composition are added or juxtaposed to other fragments, to pauses, so that the work seems always to be at the point of sinking into chaos, while it ends up with its meaning emerging. Bausch adds sound layers to the movements of dancers scattered onstage, or to groups of dancers, independent of each other, occupied with different things, while the background itself moves and transforms.

Here we are in a jungle. She even showed a jungle onstage, with dancers crossing it and merging with the lighting. They danced then as if the dance was invented to carry away the body to an adventure. Every performance is a risky voyage, an exploration.

With each new work we felt as if we were starting anew, as if we were at the beginning, each work was like a workshop, achieving a strange transparency. We were conscious, inexplicably, of the process of her mind. The same is true of her attitude toward the concept of movement itself. The dance starts with stillness, an immobility that could be full of movement. Thus, she confided in an interview: "… I look for a form which expresses simply what I feel, and suddenly this form has nothing to do with dance. Or, rather, dance is present but not shown directly. I mean that the movements are so simple one might think that it is not dance. For me, it's the opposite that is true. I think that in the people with whom I work, there is a great deal of dance, even when they are standing still."

In the end, I consider her dance-theatre to be opera, a renewal of opera. She worked well with existing operas and created for them some of her most fabulous dances. *Bluebeard* is unforgettable, so inventive, so wild, so "right." So is her *Orpheus and Eurydice*. From German expressionism to Greek tragedy she drew a straight line, thus reuniting the two poles of German thought. She did it like no one else. That is not to be explained, but must be seen. Her own creations could be considered as operas, too, because, in spite of the absence of a libretto and singers, they belong to the spirit of opera: they offer a mixture of surprising elements, outstanding music, acting that has the exaggeration opera allows, and dance is of course an integral part of the whole. Above all, there is this passion that has carried opera through the centuries, and which is present in all her work. That ecstatic effect that we expect from opera pervades her universe. In our memory, everything she did is song.

I saw her for the last time, in June 2008, on the sidewalk adjoining the Théâtre de la Ville, in Paris. I was sitting before the performance at the Café Mistral, next to the theatre. She walked in front of my table toward the corner of the square and turned to the left. She seemed to slide slowly, looking straight ahead, wearing a dress that covered her down to her ankles. She was utterly pale, her skin transparent, her eyes translucent. She looked like a ghost in motion. I felt that something in her was ended.

She looked like a distant copy of her old self in *Café Müller*. And all of *Café Müller* unfolded before my eyes, for that work is surely her archetypal creation, everything that she had simplified to the extreme, all there was to say. The subtext of all her creations is there: her secret fear of madness, her familiarity with it, because every time one reaches one's furthest limit we are dealing with madness, madness awaits us, and looks at us as a manifestation of death. In *Café Müller* her old collaborator, Madness-unto-Death, made bare, invaded the space: young people banging their heads on tables, chairs, and walls, with all their blind energies. She was dancing slowly and alone, in the corners, in the background, stretching and twisting her arms, in the shadows, like an eye, death's constant eye on the forces of life.

Death carried her away. All we can say is: Dear Pina, *auf Wiedersehen*!

(translated from the French by Bonnie Marranca)

At a Certain Hour of the Night

This play could be produced in three different ways: with two women, one older than the other; two men, one older than the other; or a man and a woman, one older than the other. The older person would be in her or his late seventies, or early eighties, and the younger would be fifty-five years old, or near that age. The text will remain the same for each case; only the grammar will have to be adjusted.

My intention is to show the oneness of love.

In a corner of the stage is a couch on which a woman is lying; she is dying. Towards the morning we hear the siren of an ambulance coming to take her dead body away. It's the end of the play.

The dialogue is taking place in a single night.

A: In this dark night we are at last reunited. But what has become of us during these long, long years … (*Turning slightly towards the couch.*) She has been lying there for a week, two weeks, dying without dying? (*Back to B.*) For how long have you been here, why did you wait so long to let me know?

B: You're always on the go, at least that was usually the case. One never knows how to find you, where, but I tried. In these last weeks she was particularly eager to see you again. "So many years," she was saying.

A: You mean I was always going away from you? Yes, I was.

B: Your timing was always wrong ... who knows, you may have been right. I can't tell anymore.

A: And you have been thinking of me, all those years?

B: These long years. Thinking of what happened to both of us.

A: You can't speak of "both of us." Why should you open such an old wound?

B: I thought of you so intensely, so much, when I received this letter, this short letter that you sent. When you heard about the fire that had devastated my whole neighborhood ... you feared for me, for us ... but we were safe, thankfully.

A: Yes, it was on national news. I was afraid that the fire had reached your home. It's true, so much time had gone by, but you were alright, comfortable in your job, in your life.

B: We're happy. Yes, I'm always happy.

A: Always, always. At the end of your letters you were adding "always." That's years ago. What did it mean? Did it mean I don't love you, but I do? Is that what it meant?

B: If it meant that you're dear to my life, yes. But where's my life? You were part of it, certainly, at the beginning, for sure, oh that light through my windows that you liked so much, your dreams, oh were you not dreaming!

A: I used to think of you even when you were standing in front of me, running away from you to meet you in my thoughts. I was quivering, I was lost. Remember, I was not twenty yet.

B: We're not going to make a tale out of our lives … Our lives. So many things have happened since. You have had involvements with so many people, how can I ignore all that.

A: I used to wait for you from the beginning of the day, waiting for the evening, waiting for you to come, go into the kitchen, prepare some meal, cross the corridor, a corridor always in the dark, and then you were telling me whatever had happened in the day.

B: And you had your big and innocent eyes, constantly discovering the world.

A: Let's start again, let's go back to those days.

B: My love, it's impossible. Do you have to be always running after the moon! You really didn't change. But are you just speaking nonsense?

A: Why do you say it's impossible?

B: You know why as much as I do.

A: Because you're "married"?

B: You're married, too. I mean you're not living alone. You never have.

A: It's not the same. It's never the same. I used to cry, every time you were going away, I was crying, for hours, in public, in my room, facing the mirror, on my pillow. Sometimes I was crying in front of you, when you behaved with indifference, when you didn't want to, you were afraid that they would find out … It took you so long to say yes to me, to admit, to be disarmed … what can I say?

B: We don't need to look back, here, now. We just met again, we may have a few hours, it's that much won … won on what, I can't tell.

A: Look at me, I live with my memories; they never leave me. And there are things I want to clarify, even now. Why were you so afraid of people, hiding, always hiding, lying, why?

B: Darling, I couldn't tell everything, I had to be careful. You were so oblivious of everything that was around us; you never noticed the suspicions, the glances that undress one's soul, the hostility that people exude against any manifestation of love.

The world can be so sordid, and it is. By now, you must have found out. I have known men and women who committed suicide because they were so humiliated by their parents, their friends, even. I wanted to shelter you, as I had been affronted all the way back during my adolescence. You used to live in a bubble, oh such a transparent one! I was admiring your innocence, and envying it too. I have to tell you, although it's still painful to admit it, that I didn't have your availability, your youth, the way you could start on the road at midnight, with just a toothbrush … I never experienced the kind of freedom that you had.

A: When you left with that awful South American young girl you didn't hide, you behaved so natural, both of you. You settled together, regardless, impervious to anything and anybody. Fearless!

B: The times had changed. Not totally, but they had.

A: How many years did you live together?

B: Not many, really. I forgot.

A: I have not forgotten. There are pains one never forgets. As I have not forgotten, either, that whiteness, that clarity of the air that you were bringing into my room, whenever, this almost blinding light that you were shedding on my days, when you were getting pale just at the sight of me, when your lower lip was quivering, is all that gone for you?

B: We were reading books together.

A: I was reading them to look for you through the words. I could barely sleep. I was deprived of you the whole length of the days.

B: Why do you bring all this up? It's so useless. It's another world, aren't you tired of the past? I don't linger on it, I haven't changed on that score.

A: And in the evening, there was your lamp, your face lit by its light, a golden glow over you, and the perfume you were putting on your fingers, and I was coming near your hands, the riches of my nights ...

B: Those were our best years—but there's nothing left.

A: I had to go and sleep alone, a few rooms away from yours. The irony that seems to have governed my life started right there, at the beginning, with love, that first sight of you, I entered your soul much before entering your body.

B: Stop it! My darling, stop it! So much time has run, like a river, like sand. You never had a clear sense of reality, going always too fast; that's by the way what I loved in you, and what I had to run away from.

A: You ran away from love. That's all.

B: But I was returning to you, and you couldn't see it. Were you in love with your own dreams? Was it rather that I was myself intimidated by you? It's too late for us to bother with such things. We're the shadows of our own past.

A: Everything is always too late. Tomorrow, you're already leaving. But our lives have left us. Years have gone and I never received a word from you, yet we were not far from each other. We are living by the same ocean ... one hour by air. So many times I looked at the sunset and told myself "she may be looking at the same scene ... and tonight she'll lie by that woman . . ." It's a marriage, I have to admit it, it has lasted so long. You had announced it to me, we were in that charming though wretched restaurant in Paris when in your cool ways you said to me that you had found the answer to your life.

B: Yes, and that's still true ... You don't have to bother, though, I loved you much before you had the slightest idea that I did. And after all, you're the one who went first, with that young woman, she was beautiful, yes, you were driving all over Europe together, fooling around while I had to rebuild myself. I never said much, then.

A: This lack of love, this uninterrupted silence ... did you ever think that it was nothing? I couldn't sleep, or otherwise was sleeping for days, because I wanted to forget you and still find you, God knows where. It's in recurring dreams that you were kissing me, as if annihilated by passion, and at the end my hands were holding nothing but smoke.

B: You're still daydreaming.

A: You were peacefully asleep. Pale. White. I have often seen you as if you were dead. You must be aware of that. White, and stretched on your bed, and withdrawn into the pity you always felt for yourself, feeding your own pain, the pain of a little girl deserted by the suicide of her mother.

B: There has always been a misunderstanding between us. I intended to protect you for the evil that I had in me.

A: Evil, what evil? Can love ever be evil? Nonsense. This so-called desire to protect me against yourself, I never bought it! I was facing an open field with so many roads, and at the end of each I was expecting to reach you, and when I was there, there was nothing. Sheer air.

B: Oh yes, I was there, but you couldn't see me. I was divided against myself and yet I was waiting for you, but was not admitting it, let alone that I didn't want you to know. You were violent, as violent as children, and little horses. There was something in you that used to scare me.

A: Now that we are leading separate lives though by the same Pacific ocean whose beauty is almost monstrous, I still consider you to be a kind of a secret, a secret I cannot decipher, with my hands as empty as ever. It's time for me to find the courage to tell you what I should have told you from the beginning. I didn't do it. I'm looking at you and you're radiating my own happiness.

Should torture be the price for the kind of bliss your presence still creates? Should I face you as a Christ become female, unveil body and soul in order to draw you to my warmth, my solar origin, you who are maleficent and moon-struck?!

Let me talk to you about my sickness, of love-sickness and lack of love. I have been unable to either put up with or forget your absence, these trains, buses, boats … all the means of voyage have been used by you to avoid me, to leave me alone on hospital beds, following a destiny which had to exclude me.

B: You always sensed that I loved you. I had such tenderness for the dear little wounded animal that you were, the dear child I couldn't keep.

A: I went out of my mind, so many times, until I wished that the summer's sun burn my eyes so that they won't try to see you again.

B: And you couldn't sleep.

A: No, I couldn't.

B: Although . . .

A: Although . . .

B: You were having affairs, you were traveling … not answering my letters.

A: And why?

B: Why?

A: Because your letters were informing me that you were riding horses in Montana; your letters from Ohio and New York State were telling that your odious partner was going on painting her awful canvases, that you loved her narrow hips, and so on, while I was waiting for the first break between you, and the split eventually happened, and you suffered like hell, I heard, she left and I wished you a pain until death, and you didn't ask me to come back.

B: Always speaking of death, always these inflated statements.

A: There's nothing overblown in what I say, I'm speaking of pain, real pain, the one which settles in one's bones. Forever.

B: Death, always death, I say. (*Looking towards the couch.*) Look, we're like this woman, she moves, she's giving a fight, she refuses to die. She's near the end.

A: She can't love anybody anymore. She's lucky. Sleeping … But you loved her too, though it didn't last. She remained faithful to you. She was obsessed by you. She also loved me, in some way. And somehow I was looking for you in her presence but it was useless. I ended up feeling a strange kind of disgust. Soft tenderness is really not for me.

B: We are probably the keepers of some hidden thing, something I have never figured out totally. I have never understood the nature of what was attaching me to you. The word love must have scared me.

A: We're in a strange place, in a strange moment. Will her agony keep going?

B: At least she doesn't seem to suffer. We'll find out soon. Anyway, I won't wait here for ever.

A: You're sleeping here? Of course not.

B: We're already late in the night. I wonder …

A: You were never telling me ahead of time that you were planning to leave. You were running away like a thief. Always hiding something. Always lying. Women also can be cowards. That's what you have always been. And I fell for that! I did. Good Lord, I did.

B: You're again turning in circles. Do you want me to tell you that you used to make it hard for me to do almost anything. Things were always going wrong.

A: To leave without a word, without a tear.

B: Yes. I never cry. Oh, it may not be so true. You didn't need see me crying. But stop it. We're getting nowhere.

A: Our lives are done. It all went fast, like those days in the countryside, when, come evening, the baskets are put aside, and everyone plunges in the melancholy of the return.

B: We kiss each other goodbye and the other is already not listening. You were projected into the future, residing I never knew where, incapable to still your mind on the here and now. There was nothing I could do.

A: Does all our talking make any sense? (*A moves very close to B.*)

B: Don't come that close to me … you will disturb her.

A: She mustn't be hearing a thing! Feel nothing! God knows where she is. But I'm here, listen

B: (*Pulling back a bit.*) Not here!

A: I wanted to kiss your hands … Just your hands.

B: My hands have aged.

A: You're shaking all over. I know what goes on in you when you start shaking. You denied it, but when you were shaking it meant you desired me.

B: No! Not here, not now!

A: Then, where? Never?

B: Maybe not. Oh yes, never.

A: But why?

B: You can't discuss love in the room of a dying person. It's sheer madness.

A: She's not dead. She's sleeping. Maybe more deeply than a while ago. And us, where will we meet tomorrow? Tomorrow? Tomorrow where?

B: Tomorrow I will have to catch my plane. For us, as you say, it's too late. You're daydreaming, nothing changed. My dearest, we can never restart things, never.

A: It's over. Every drop of my blood knows that it's over, and for decades. But nothing ever ends. Death, is, for sure, a kind of an end, but we don't understand it. I don't even realize where I stand, right now. It's all a big cloud. But you have been like a source of light that I loved more than love. And you will tell me that all this is finished?!

B: Nothing ends, for sure. But can I make you sense how weary I am. I am tired. I am weary. I am an old woman. Face it.

A: (*Turns towards the couch.*) Look at her, look! You will be lying one day soon on your deathbed, like she does, and as you excluded me for so long from paradise, I will not be there to close your eyes.

B: I protected you against myself, I repeat. I never dared tell you all the miseries I had endured before I met you.

A: The destruction of a heart is worst than the destruction of nations. You destroyed me. Your arguments mean nothing.

B: The truth is I wanted to keep your friendship.

A: While I wanted to keep our nights. A life together.

B: I guess so. It was impossible.

A: And why?

B: We are here. At long last. Let's have a moment of peace.

A: We are here and it's a disaster.

B: She's hardly breathing. We're supposed to watch over her. She won't last. She was a courageous woman, I would say an admirable one.

A: Yes, she will die. We are surrounded by death, I mean us, yes, we have always been. We had this thing in common, a mother who was a kept woman, an only child who had to absorb her anguish; her love, too. You were twelve and you came home from school, at noon, I think, and found her in a pool of her blood, a suicide. A little gun by her side. You always stopped the story at the presence of the gun.

B: You remember it . . .

A: In that funereal chamber that my memory has become I keep everything that's related to you. I live with your ghost, I sleep with your ghost, near me, around me, under me, suffocating and tender, love of my love.

B: What are you really trying to do? We came to see for the last time a dying friend. That's all.

A: We're all alone. This dark night which is all around is also within our heads. I will teach you something before you yourself soon become some fire, some dust, that by the way I will myself breathe, while you will be lost for the whole of the universe. I will inform you of a basic truth about you, the fact that your life got extinguished the very day you gave up on me ... ever since, we have been survivors, candles set aside, dead leaves, dead lands.

B: What happened will always have happened. Nothing can take it back from us.

A: I know. Those sweeping statements are empty shells. Don't I recognize you in them!

B: I loved the child in you; oh those innocent eyes that were looking at me, where are they? This feeling of guilt, a woman's guilt, made me resent you. I resented your very existence; you came to me as a luxury I was both entitled to, and couldn't afford. It was tough. I was living in such an utter insecurity and you were impervious to my reality, as well as to yours, in fact. It was unfair, but that's the way it was. And I have never said it before, I was jealous of you, terribly jealous of your capacity for passion, even if it were addressed to me. There was also this strange desire I used to feel, this need to die for you so as to be reborn for others. It's always for the sake of some other person that one recovers from one's love.

A: So you consider yourself as being cured.

B: Wait a moment. (*B goes to the couch.*) She's really dying. Not any noise. This silence, this sadness … There's nothing we can do. We should think of her. Mourn her. I should say some prayer, but I never learned how to do that.

A: So you're admitting that we're caught in death's circular and irresistible movement. She's dying, this woman is dying, is gone, and me too, and both of us. She has brought us together, and she will separate us. We will soon go again our separate ways, pretending to live. She gave us, though, our last chance.

B: She had been so fond of you. You were an enchantment for her.

A: Listen to me. We have no present, no future. Don't tell me you never loved me, that's nonsense. I can't help it. I love you!

B: . . . .

A: I must dry your tears, they don't need to see them when they will come. They will separate us forever.

B: There's one last thing you must know about me. I have never been able to love anybody unreservedly. To love totally, no, never. Let's forget all this talk. The ambulance must be on its way. They will carry her not to her home, no, to the morgue.

A: Now, listen carefully. I'm insisting, listen! When the ambulance will be gone with her, we will leave together. It's our last chance. I'm clear about it. This time, I'm not going to lose you. Come what come, we'll go together, somewhere, we'll find out.

B: You're out of your mind. Where do you want us to go? You have your life, and I have mine.

A: You have nothing, and I have nothing. There are hotels, there are trains. We'll find a room. We'll let the walls close in on us. I have to feel that between you and me there will be no place anymore for anything whatsoever, not for a needle. The doors of hell will open. We shall at last live.

B: It's impossible.

A: Let's have one night, two nights … Later, you'll have an eternity of a night all to yourself … let's have a few days of real happiness, a few days stolen from the gods, from pain, how can you refuse? Nothing else should matter.

B: You're insane. You're scaring me.

A: Is wanting to live unreasonable? I seldom spoke my mind to you, and that must have been a fatal error. Now, I will be forceful. I am begging, begging you to listen, let's go! Say that we will go together, anyway you want.

B: It's totally out of the question.

A: We'll discover some place together. Be totally anony-mous. By a beach. I will teach you every evening a new sunset. It will be as you like. We will laugh, will forget time, people, everything. We will speak for hours, you will tell me things you told no one. Remember, you were telling me, over and over, "I want to speak to you, oh how I need speak to you," and it really never happened. It still haunts me. Now, it's time to do what you really always wanted to do.

B: I want none of all that. I am not as unhappy as you think. I am satisfied with my life. You have no idea.

A: It's beside the point. I am asking you to give us what we missed. Missed. Lost. Give yourself a moment of truth. Before your turn comes for disappearing from this world give yourself some moments of true happiness, be free!

B: I will never be able to go away with you. I can't. I don't want to. You have to believe me.

A: (*A big silence. A pounds the wall with her fists.*) Therefore, what if we take right away, here and now, the decision to die? Not willing to live together, we shall die together ... I am inviting you to a grand voyage! You will repeat this trip that you took to the sea in order to join me; you did it twice, three times, and each time to return after the worst kinds of misunderstandings. But now, we'll return right there, if you would die with me, our ghosts will find that fateful room. That last voyage, we will have to do it anyway, sooner maybe than we think, so let's do it together, let's retrieve our love in a long moment made eternal by our common death. You don't want to live with me, so you will die with me.

B: You are tearing me apart, my love.

A: Daylight will come soon. Let it rise for us too. In death we'll find a new life.

B: You're delirious. Totally out of your mind.

A. I already told you that I always thought you were a coward! Why are you afraid of dying since you're already dead? Should I stir your memories again and again? During one of our nights you had whispered to my ear: "I am dead," and you cried, the only time I saw you cry, defeated at last. You had asked me not to move, to remain calm, like the surface of a pond, and suddenly you plunged in the dark water, possessed all my senses, and I had to shout, then the pond rescinded itself, and I didn't know if I was with an angel or a being made of flesh, if my spirit was not breaking even more than my body under the weight of a total bliss. "Close your eyes," you were asking, and I was closing them, I was hurting at the edge of your love, of your life, and you were breathing my own breath. How, but how and where to, has all this disappeared?

B: Yes, I was a being of the night, and still am. But in my nights things didn't go well. In them, I was encountering mostly vultures, storms, terror, cataclysms. I had tried so many times to tell you about it but you were never listening. Now we can't allow ourselves any great upheavals.

A: You and I came here, mind you, to watch a grand rehearsal. We're here to see her dying, lying over there, to see how people die, as we will also die, soon, together, after all these years.

B: It's hard for me to see you suffer to this point. Stop it. Please.

A: I will explain to you death's meaning. You will listen.

B: Not now. Not here. It's suffocating.

A: When you don't want to suffocate anymore you must accept to die.

B: We won't have to wait any longer.

A: The more I look at you the more I get what's happening to me. I suddenly am in love with death. I hunger for it, I yearn for it as if it were a dessert, I feel a desire for it as if she were a woman, she is possessing me as you would have, she resembles you, she's so beautiful, she's here and you will share her with me, she's splendid madness …

B: It's hard to hear you, to see you suffer … They will be here in a matter of seconds … Can you be out of reality to such a degree?

A: The dead have a new soul, different from the one they had while living. Death has an intensity with which I am familiar and that will inhabit me from now on. It's a dark stream circulating in the arteries, alongside one's blood. This intensity belonged to life and we refused it. Now I wonder if death isn't a kind of life in its own right, if there isn't a joy that belongs particularly to death, if death doesn't originate in the divine, like love itself. Let me speak to you of love now that we're nearing our end. Give up your ridiculous defenses and face things as they are. Allow me to tell you that love befriends only life and death. We have rejected the one, we shall embrace the other. And you won't have the freedom of choice. For the first, and last time, you will have to follow me, you will, all the way to the end. I, at last, finally took power over you, and that road is irreversible.

B: If only I could help you! If you could only realize how much you meant to me, and still do. How much it nearly destroyed me to let you go. You don't need to push me towards my death, time will do it. It's just a question of numbers. You're looking at me but not hearing. I am at your mercy, you have to believe me.

A: I waited too long for this moment to happen so I won't let it go! I maintained in its perfect state a maddening love for you that you were dreading, that you thought was forbidden, that you were hiding from, though after you left me you ignored these fears and scruples. Now you will do exactly as I say. We missed the possibility to live together, we will do it now, and in death. Mixed together forever. If you could be outside, you will see that the sky has cleared. Until infinity.

B: I said you scare me, and you do.

A: It's time you're scared.

B: But I am here, at your mercy, as usual.

A: Ta ta ta … You will follow me down the scales to hell, in the dark, in the cold. You will never desert me.

B: I'm hearing the ambulance's siren. They have arrived. They will soon open this door. They'll take her away. It's quite a while since she has died, but you don't want to know it. I wish that they let some air in this room. We badly need it. You may come back a little to your senses.

A: Let the dead take care of the dead. They can come and take her away; I will take care of us.

B: If only you could at last see how worn out I am! I am really exhausted. And there isn't much left in me to lose. My journey is done. You want to do as you please, do it. My energies are too far gone for me to resist. You may be right, who knows … and who cares? Nothing makes sense anymore. So let it be.

A: As soon as they will be out of here, I will push you into my car and we will go, like in the past, like when we crossed together the whole of this continent, I will drive straight ahead and you will keep quiet, you will obey our common destiny, I know where we're going, I am taking you to the sea, the sea that I love and that you hate, the sun will be barely out, you will not mind that they will see us, you won't have to be a coward anymore, and we will reach the cliff, this time you will say yes to everything I decide, absolutely everything, and any way I can't care less if you agree or not, you will obey me, to death, and the car will go over the cliff, and they will later find us together, and when they will look they won't be able to know whose hand is this, and whose eye is that, to whom these bloody hearts used to belong, and I will tell them, from death's other side, that all this mess they see is us, it's you and me, indistinctly, that we are this heap of flesh and bones, and that at last nothing will ever be able to separate us. Nothing.

Queen of the Sea

The sea moves in our lips and
rises as walls in our eyes

the wind disturbs our hair
to turn it into spikes and
thorns

here it is as a palm on the
pacified backbone of the waters

eternity runs on the fluidity
of matter, neither movement
nor essence but the washed and
washed out visage of the sea

I am exposed to the nudity of light
and abandoned to the multiple lip
of the sea

I am liquid   liquid element
the earth   its volcanoes   its canyons   its wrath

I am its torrents   its slime   its silt
and its spring

liquid   liquid element
I am the sea and united to the sea

Crime of Honor

Characters
A Nun
A young Girl
The Mother
A young man, Hussein

PROLOGUE

1ST PERSON: I wonder. Has she paid him back?

2ND PERSON: Who knows? We're not even sure she's still around.

1ST PERSON: Has she seen him after that scene?

2ND PERSON: She must have. They worked in the same office.

1ST PERSON: What a strange story. They must all be gone by now.

2ND PERSON: There's no way for us to know.

SCENE I

GIRL, NUN

(*A classroom. A blackboard. Great silence.*)

(*On a low platform, sitting on a chair, a NUN, shuffling some notes, getting ready for class. A young GIRL enters, eighteen years old. She deposits on the desk an enormous bouquet of lilies, a box of sugar-coated almonds, and a smaller box. The nun is flabbergasted. Opening the box of white almonds then looking again at the white lilies, she exclaims.*)

SISTER: But that's a marriage!

(*Silence.*)

(*She opens the small box. She brings out a beautiful watch, round and flat, like the one rich men used to carry in a special pocket. Feeling embarrassed.*)

SISTER: What's this?! It's too beautiful. How can I accept such an expensive gift! What have you done!

GIRL: (*Standing speechless.*)

SISTER: How do you want me to accept that. You're too extravagant. It's against the rules of the convent for us to accept expensive gifts. Why did you do that?

GIRL: They told me it's your birthday today.

SISTER: My birthday, yes. But you're a foolish little girl. What can I say in front of all this. Besides, it's not one present, it's an avalanche!

GIRL: You need a watch. I know it, so I found one. And anyway, I wanted to give you a present. It's yours.

SISTER: It's overwhelming. We're not allowed to receive such gifts. You spent a fortune. Why did you?

GIRL: You know I attend school in the morning, then work in an office. It's my own money.

SISTER: (*Looking at the watch.*) It's so beautiful, yes, but it's too much, too much. I'm speechless.

GIRL: You do receive crates and crates of oranges and mandarins from Yolanda. Everybody pampers her, has eyes only for her, and that makes her so arrogant. I can't stand her. I can give presents too. I want to say something.

SISTER: My child, those crates are sent by her parents to the convent, not to me. They have big properties, and they're so generous. But personally, I have nothing to do with them.

GIRL: But you do like HER?

SISTER: She's in our boarding school, feeling so lonely sometimes. We love all our students. You know that.

GIRL: I am not "all" the students.

SISTER: I can't make exceptions.

GIRL: I am not asking for …

SISTER: I know. (*Holding the watch carefully.*) I have to admit. It's a beautiful watch. I will try to keep it, I promise, but I'll have to check with the Mother Superior. She may give me the permission, and she may not. I'll do my best, I promise.

GIRL: You must keep it.

SISTER: When we enter the convent we take vows of poverty, we renounce luxury.

GIRL: But this is just a useful object.

SISTER: This is too much. You're very dear to me, I don't need to repeat it, but I should rather be angry. How can you be so foolish!

GIRL: But it's your birthday!

SISTER: Yes, it is my birthday, I appreciate it, I do, but I wish you were more reasonable. What can I say?! I worry for you. You're so excessive. I have told you that quite a few times. Please, be reasonable.

GIRL: I am reasonable, and I am lonely too.

SISTER: I feel it. This is not the time to dramatize things. We spoke already about your relations with your Mother. I have been so patient. In fact, I shouldn't, but I told you I have a special place for you in my heart. I mention you in my prayers. You have nothing to fear. And I don't need special presents to care for you.

GIRL: That's not the point. I wanted to create a special moment for you. Something beautiful. Something nobody else would do. And I am not poor.

SISTER: This IS extraordinary. How can I thank you? But you're a child, a dear one, and so foolish. You disarm me.

(*A bell rings for classes to start.*)

SISTER: Class must be starting soon. I will take the flowers to the chapel. Stay here.

(*SISTER exits, taking everything on the table with her.*)

SCENE II

GIRL, MOTHER

MOTHER: There was money in this drawer, and it's gone. You must have stolen it!

GIRL: How can I steal it? I didn't.

MOTHER: But of course you did.

GIRL: I didn't. I tell you I didn't. What would I do with it?!

MOTHER: There's only your father, me and you, in this house. And the money was in this drawer. I put it in with my own hands just three days ago. I prepared it to pay the rent, and some other things. It was all prepared, and now it's gone. You will have to tell me where it is because you're the only one who knows. Where is it?

GIRL: I don't know. I didn't do it.

MOTHER: Listen. I counted the money and put it here, in this drawer. And nobody visited the house since. It could only be you, nobody else entered this room. I am not a fool.

GIRL: I don't know how it disappeared. I can't do much.

MOTHER: You can return it.

GIRL: How? I don't have it.

MOTHER: You will stay in this room until you tell me where's this money. I will lock you in if you don't talk.

GIRL: (*Panicked.*) I don't have the money.

MOTHER: You must have taken it and hid it somewhere.

GIRL: I haven't hidden it.

MOTHER: So where is it?

GIRL: I don't know.

MOTHER: You sure know. Now, sit down and tell me.

(*The MOTHER pulls the GIRL on a sofa and sits next to her.*)

GIRL: What would I tell you?

MOTHER: You know perfectly well what you have to say.

GIRL: If I told you I didn't ?!

MOTHER: You won't say that. You stole the money and now you'll have to give it back.

GIRL: I haven't stolen the money. I really don't have it.

MOTHER: You don't have it? Where is it then?

GIRL: I don't know.

MOTHER: This cannot go on.

GIRL: I have given it.

MOTHER: Given it? To whom?

GIRL: I have not given it. I lent it.

MOTHER: So you took something which isn't yours and gave it away? You're a thief. This money has to come back to where it was. The sooner the better. And where is it now? You lent it to whom?

GIRL: Don't call me a thief, Mother.

MOTHER: Whoever steals is a thief.

GIRL: I can't answer you.

MOTHER: Don't look so terrified. You just tell me to whom you lent it, and I will get it back.

GIRL: Oh no, no!

MOTHER: So who is it?

GIRL: I lent it to Hussein, at the office. He needed to borrow money, and I gave it to him.

MOTHER: To Hussein? That horrible man who says he wants to marry you? You know that I told him once, once and for all, to stop chasing you, I have no daughter for him.

GIRL: I don't want to marry him, him or anybody else, that's sure. You don't need to worry.

MOTHER: He keeps pestering you. And I have news for you. Your Hussein is a murderer. He killed his sister. He should have been hanged.

GIRL: Hussein, a murderer! It's impossible. How can you say such a terrible thing? He's poor, but he's decent. He is the nicest person I know.

MOTHER: Hussein, nice? Of course he won't tell you. But I know it. My neighbor told me that, by the way just recently. That guy killed his sister. And they put him in prison. How did they hire him in your office, mixing criminals with young girls!

GIRL: How can you say such a thing about Hussein. I don't love him, no, but he's so helpless, so kind … the gentlest soul one can imagine.

MOTHER: Gentlest soul? A thief, a gouger of money. He takes money from women, he's a pimp, a criminal pimp, that's what he is.

GIRL: I never heard that he killed his sister. What a horror! It must be a lie, a big lie. He's the most gentle of all the employees, I swear. And nobody ever said anything to me against him. What you just said is scary. I can't believe it. I'll ask him.

MOTHER: They tell me that when it happened it was all over the papers. I must have been visiting my in-laws in Damascus, and missed the news. The whole city was shaken as they told me his brother is in politics, a politician, it fits. A guy from a family of killers! But you won't have to ask him anything. I will be the one to deal with him. He won't escape my wrath. That, I promise. Too bad it's getting late now. Tomorrow, just after my doctor's appointment, I'm going to the office to confront him. He won't get away with it. He better give my money back, or I will be the one to land him in jail once again.

GIRL: You won't.

MOTHER: Of course I will. That money has to come back, I need it.

SCENE III

GIRL, HUSSEIN

(*At the office.*)

GIRL: Hussein, I have to talk to you.

HUSSEIN: What is it? You're looking so nervous; something must be bothering you.

GIRL: I have to tell you quickly, we don't have much time. A few days ago I had to give a gift and I took money from the house and my Mother found out. She's out of her mind, ready to kill me.

HUSSEIN: You took money for a gift? A lot of money?

GIRL: One hundred and twenty-five pounds.

HUSSEIN: That's really a lot of money. More than a month's salary. What did you do with it?

GIRL: I bought a watch for the Sister at school.

HUSSEIN: A watch, for whom?

GIRL: The Sister at school. My teacher.

HUSSEIN: The Sister?

GIRL: Yes.

HUSSEIN: That's too much money for a gift. I don't understand. Did you need to do that?

GIRL: I did.

HUSSEIN: I don't understand. Do you love her that much?

GIRL: Love her? What a question. I want her to care for me, yes. But that's not the point. She's my philosophy teacher, I wish you knew her, she's … not like everybody else. I hate the nuns, well, I don't care, but she's different. Different, I mean it. It's because of her that I can both work and go to school. She made all the arrangements.

HUSSEIN: And you're shaking. You took money from your parents to please her?

GIRL: I consider it as my money, but my Mother doesn't see it that way. She takes all my salary, every month, as soon as I get it, it has been like that since I went to work. Gives me a pittance. "Pocket money," she says, "is enough." I can't buy two sandwiches with what she gives me back.

HUSSEIN: Talk with her.

GIRL: Talk? You met her. She's crazy, as wild as a beast. I have to tell you … she asked what I did with this money and I couldn't tell her the truth. If she knew, nothing would stop her. She would go to the school and shame me in front of everybody, make a scene. I will lose face, and she will accuse the Sister of all sorts of things, give her hell. I would rather die!

HUSSEIN: You're in a bad situation, but what can I do?

GIRL: I told her that you borrowed that money from me.

HUSSEIN: You said that?!

GIRL: Yes. And I beg you, beg you to tell her that you did, when she will confront you.

HUSSEIN: You know I love you. I do. I would marry you, I said it so many times. But I live on my salary which isn't much, and I don't have any money to spare. How can I face her. Will she ask to be reimbursed. Oh God!

GIRL: I think she will. I know she will.

HUSSEIN: I would have willingly, but I'm broke

GIRL: Hussein, please, listen. When I was seven or eight years old, the school mistress had distributed dolls to the class, naked dolls. We were supposed to take them home, make dresses for them, and return them for a charity sale. On the way home I broke my doll and felt ashamed. There was a shiny coin of twenty-five piasters on the table, I took it and went to the store and bought a brand new doll all dressed up in blue. I remember. The school mistress was surprised, but she thanked me. And there in the middle of the lesson, my Mother appeared. She entered as a storm, dragged me by the hair out of the classroom while shouting that I was a thief. The school mistress tried to calm her down. The story of the broken doll was uncovered. I wished then the ground broke under my feet and swallowed me. I suffered for the rest of the school year from that humiliation. All the kids heard that I was a thief, they all knew that I was a child beaten. The memory of that day still bothers me.

HUSSEIN: In what kind of a world are you living? So much fear …

GIRL: Now, if she found out the truth, she will, as I told you, go and retrieve the watch and humiliate me again, in front of the whole school, and humiliate the Sister too … I rather see her walk on my dead body than go through all that. I just can't.

HUSSEIN: She must be so mean, so impossibly hard.

GIRL: You have no idea.

HUSSEIN: She's coming here, you mean, at the office?

GIRL: Anytime now.

HUSSEIN: What do you expect me to do?

GIRL: Well … She's out of her mind. And she also said that you murdered your sister.

HUSSEIN: She told you what, that I murdered my sister? People are still saying that? Good Lord, that's not true, not true. I did not kill my sister. Where did she hear that? I have already paid enough for a lie, will that mess follow me for ever and never stop?!

GIRL: She's really mean, as you said. Her neighbor told her those things about you that upset her, and she's bringing them out right now. She must have invented that story. It's a lie, for sure, out of her terrible ability to fantasize.

HUSSEIN: We'll talk about that later. I wish I didn't need to explain to you the whole story, but I will have to. I'll explain to you what really happened. But first I swear on all the things that are dear to me, and that includes you, you the most important one, that I am not a killer. You have to believe me. Believe me. Otherwise I will be more destroyed than I already am.

GIRL: Listen, you can't let me down. You can't. I beg you. I'm sorry, but it's done. Don't ever tell Mother that you didn't borrow that money, don't, don't!

HUSSEIN: You're facing me with a big problem, I can't betray you, I never will, but it's hard, all I have is the money here in my pocket, here, that's all I have, it will get me barely to the month's end ... nothing more.

GIRL: I'm looking you in the eye, Hussein. I have no choice but to beg you for help. I will never ask you again for any favor, I promise, but this time ...

HUSSEIN: Please don't cry.

GIRL: Listen, listen, Good Lord she's here, I heard her voice. Yes, here she is.

SCENE IV

MOTHER, HUSSEIN, GIRL

(*At the Office.*)

MOTHER: Here you are, the two of you. And here I am.

HUSSEIN: Yes.

MOTHER: You borrowed money from my daughter?

HUSSEIN: Yes and no.

MOTHER: What do you mean by yes and no? She stole money from me to give it to you.

GIRL: I did not steal. How can I say it, but it's my money too.

MOTHER: What do you mean your money too?

GIRL: I earn it, don't I?

MOTHER: Your money is my money. I raised you for all these years. And good girls give their earnings home. That's the rule in my book. And in that case, you stole from me, from my own drawer.

GIRL: No!

MOTHER: Sure you did, and let me speak. (*Addressing HUS-SEIN.*) She told me very clearly that you borrowed money from her, and you just have to give back that money that belongs to me.

HUSSEIN: I did not borrow any money, well, I don't have any money to give back.

MOTHER: Not have any money? You're a pimp and a murderer.

HUSSEIN: Wait a minute, Madam, I'm neither the one nor the other. I am an honest man.

MOTHER: I don't care what you think you are. I want one hundred and twenty-five pounds back from you, that's all. It's very simple.

HUSSEIN: Well. Give me time. I don't have any money.

MOTHER: You kill your sister, you take money from my daughter, and what else?

HUSSEIN: Let's clear things right away. I did not kill my sister. I will tell it for the first time, it's my brother that killed her.

GIRL: Your brother …

HUSSEIN: Let me settle this matter once for all. It was four years ago. My sister had spent the night outside my parents' house. She returned at dawn, just when the sun was about to rise, she tried to come home before anyone would have awaken. But my father was not sleeping. My brother too was not sleeping. They were waiting. They heard her come in, and my brother picked up his razor, and opened the door. He let her in, and in the entrance, right there, he slit her throat. I can't tell you more about how it all happened, but I heard a long, prolonged cry, then a heavy sound, and I was on my feet, I saw her on the floor in a pool of blood. My father was there, watching over the scene; he stood over the body, and in a short while, he looked at my brother and said: "You did what you had to do. I am proud of you." I think they were already suspicious, and they trapped her. They executed her with the same coldness as the razor's.

GIRL: It's too awful to be true.

HUSSEIN: My mother joined us. She looked at the floor and fainted. Father took her into their room. She shouted and shouted and he locked her in. Her voice though was piercing the walls. I could hear her, talking to herself. She was seeing blood, she was describing the murder … she saw it all. Imagine, she saw it. She was saying that they killed her daughter like they kill a chicken in the village; that her blood was running from under the door into the street, like garbage, like mud. It was going in the gutters. Imagine! "Her blood is going to feed the rats," she was telling "to feed the rats!" She was shouting, then moaning, then there were cries, then silence, cries and silence … what a terror!

Father was worried that the neighbors would hear her. He then had a long talk with my brother. We, the three of us, sat in the living room. It didn't take much time before they told me that they had decided this one thing, before calling the police; that as my brother had a brilliant political career in front of him and that as I myself was not yet legally an adult, they will tell the authorities that I was the one who had killed her. They told me coldly, with a neutral tone of voice that still sends shivers on my back, that my sentence would be a reduced one as I was a minor and that I had no choice but to obey. So ultimately I was sentenced for three years in prison with no appeal. In the courthouse, after hearing my sentence, my father took me in his arms for the first time in his life and said: "Hussein, I am proud of you. Our honor is saved."

MOTHER: What honor? Whose honor? If what you say is true, it's even worse than what I have learned. That's what they call a crime of honor in this country. It's despicable. How can crime and honor be pronounced together? Such an hypocrisy!

HUSSEIN: I paid for the family's honor I had to. But I am innocent. At least I am at peace with myself.

MOTHER: At peace? To see your sister in a pool of blood so that your brother can strut like a peacock! Some politician, that guy. A murderer and a coward, let me tell you. Is there any honor in a cold-blooded killing, let me ask? Kill somebody of your own blood, to save what? What do you mean by honor? Your honesty, your courage, your hard work, or the virginity of a poor girl who followed her instinct, those instincts that the very God we worship has created in us?! If my daughter ever runs with someone I will take that young man by the neck, and force him to marry her. But kill her, or have her killed, oh no, never, never. How did your Mother ever sleep after that sacrifice, because it was a primitive, beastly sacrifice—a sacrificial ceremony.

HUSSEIN: She didn't sleep. Her life was split between visits to the prison I was committed to, and nights of prayers. She seldom even now utters a word.

MOTHER: So you killed her too.

HUSSEIN: In a way, you are right, they did kill her too.

MOTHER: There is no honor involved in this matter, but cruelty. Bestiality. Abominable arrogance. A man can run away with any woman, marry into any religion he wants, and his will is accepted. But a woman! She's less than an object, a piece of flesh, a slave. In the eyes of people like you, the mothers of your children are worthless, allowed no will of their own, no honor! What about the real honor of these women, their responsibility, their word, their body and their soul?! Is all that nothing?

HUSSEIN: I'm not the one who made the rules. They are of our society.

MOTHER: They are not. Governments don't approve of it, although they are cowards in their own way and swim through many waters. And no holy book says that a woman has to be slaughtered because she spent a night outside her home … and who is to tell what happened when she was out? You killed her like you would an animal, a cow, a dog.

HUSSEIN: I didn't do it.

MOTHER: Your brother did. Your father did. This society did. And then you go to mosques and churches, to a God that told you "You shall not kill," you bury an innocent woman, blood of your blood, daughter and sister, how much closer can anyone be, and you dare speak of honor? Who can be more hypocritical than you?

HUSSEIN: It would have been hard for us to face our society.

MOTHER: In this case society would perhaps have not known it. You must have satisfied some obscure need to slaughter. Shame on you! And the society that accepts this kind of a murder is rotten, totally wrong. Shame on it as well.

HUSSEIN: I didn't have a word to say. I was faced with it.

MOTHER: And you paid for something you didn't do?

HUSSEIN: I had no choice, I repeat.

MOTHER: This type of slaughtering of women has to stop. These are criminal deeds, not honorable ones. And those who teach or perpetuate such laws are criminals. Subhuman.

HUSSEIN: I can't by myself change these unwritten laws.

MOTHER: You can at least regret them. You can join those of us who are against them. You can at least admit that they are a bunch of lies covering up the egos of defeated males, the egos of cowards who kill in the dark, just to feel great and powerful, and all they do is to refuse ways to be otherwise truly honorable.

HUSSEIN: Madam, I'm exhausted. I am innocent, though I paid, I paid, I paid. Prison was not easy, to say the least. It was hell.

MOTHER: But you don't seem to have learned much through your ordeal. You come out of prison and then what do you do? You take money from young girls!

HUSSEIN: Madam, let's not go back to where we started. I cannot bear much of anything of this sort.

MOTHER: You're maybe saying the truth. I don't really care. But this time you have to pay back something you really owe. You're not a victim. You have to pay what has been taken from ME.

GIRL: Mother, stop it. He's exhausted, he will collapse

MOTHER: You better shut up. I will stop when I am paid back. That's all I'm asking for.

HUSSEIN: Please don't harass me any further. I WILL pay you back. I'm broke.

MOTHER: When? Right now?

HUSSEIN: I just said that I'm broke.

MOTHER: So what?

HUSSEIN: I … I spent that money. I will give it to you by installments, I will, I give you my word.

MOTHER: When did you have the time to spend it? Anyway, it's none of my business. But I can ask: what's the worth of your word?

HUSSEIN: You have to believe me. I give you my word. It's all I have.

MOTHER: This whole thing is not right.

HUSSEIN: It's all I can do.

MOTHER: Well, you don't give me much of a choice. So we agree. You will start to pay me back by the end of this month. And I say not later. You have to keep your word, I mean it, otherwise, you won't escape, you'll hear from me, I will go to your boss in this very office, place a hold on your salary, and you will be thrown out of your job. Nobody has fooled me yet.

SCENE V

HUSSEIN, GIRL

(*At the same place.*)

GIRL: My Mother is ruthless. I have seen how terrible she has been. I'm sorry. I am deeply sorry. She's like that. But I thank you. I mean it. You saved me

HUSSEIN: I love you. I will never repeat it enough. For your sake, I will keep my word to your Mother, although I don't know how I'll manage. It will be difficult.

GIRL: I love you too, but it's not the same. I will never marry you. I have to be honest. I don't want to get married. I can't tell you why, exactly. I have never been free, and can't see myself facing new obligations. I want space in front of my eyes, uncertainty, if you want to put it that way, no ties, nothing. I'm so controlled at home, it's suffocating. There isn't much I can do. But you're noble Hussein, I would have never believed that you murdered your sister. It's a terrible story. I like you even more.

HUSSEIN: You will never figure out how hard it has been. I don't want you to know. Your Mother has been tough, but she has shaken me from a long sleep. You see, I have put up with prison because I repeated to myself, over and over, that the family had to do what it did. And still, my brother never visited me, not once! He ignored me. My father never showed any sympathy for my predicament. They behaved as if everything was alright. And it wasn't.

GIRL: You mean they never cared, though they were the ones, in a way, eho put you to jail.

HUSSEIN: They didn't. My brother got married soon after, and moved out. Now, I have to read the papers to find out how well he's doing in his politics. How famous he's becoming. When it comes to my father, it's even worse. He goes to the store, every morning. As if nothing happened. But something has happened, a dreadful thing. When he goes by in the street, God knows what they think of him. Do they pity him, how would I know? They see a killing in our house, a murder, blood within its walls. They usually thrive on such stories, it enter- tains them; anyway, the damage is done, even if they approve what we call a crime of honor. A crime it is, I see it, a crime of the worst kind. Families taking the law into their hands. The most primitive of all killings.

GIRL: Your poor father, how is he?

HUSSEIN: It's hard to tell. Never a word. He's silent, as usual. Probably more than ever, if that's possible. You can't get a word out from him. That man is a tomb all by himself.

GIRL: So he never talks with you?

HUSSEIN: Not really, as I just said. One or two words, once in a while. In jail, they were at least talking! Day and night.

GIRL: I had no idea … It's awful.

HUSSEIN: My Mother, yes, she came regularly to the prison on visiting days. And each time she cried, like the other women, and each time she said God forgive them! She's still numb. Lifeless. When she roams in the house from room to room like a ghost, I try to avoid looking at her. It's a constant heartbreak.

GIRL: You must forget, Hussein. Forget, and maybe forgive. They used you, I can see that. But you are free. You must look ahead. And you're my friend.

HUSSEIN: You know, I miss my sister. It's the first time that I'm saying it clearly. I am at last admitting it. It took me time, but I do. She was one year younger than me, we were like twins. We played games. Oh very few, the house was always so quiet. It was as if she and I were on one side of a barrier, and the rest of the family on the other. I think that my Mother was even jealous of our closeness,

GIRL: You're going through all this nightmare and I didn't know. You never opened your heart to me.

HUSSEIN: How could I have done it? And burden you with my own miseries.

GIRL: I'm sorry. Sorry. You can't imagine how sorry I am, discovering all this.

HUSSEIN: You seem to have a miserable life also, though you're so alive, so lovable. You bring joy to this whole place.

GIRL: You have seen it, you saw unfortunately how hard, how violent my Mother can get. It's a day-to-day problem. My father is the ghost of what he had been. Nobody listens to anybody at home. We are three strangers under the same roof.

HUSSEIN: Talking about my sister, I was sharing the room with her, since I was born. We were inseparable, but before her death, in the middle of some nights, I felt a few times that she was getting out of her bed and leaving ,,, I paid no attention, thinking I was dreaming. But it was true and they have found out and their awful decision was taken.

GIRL: So they killed her cold-bloodedly. It wasn't a spontaneous reaction. They knew what they were doing. They had prepared for it?

HUSSEIN: Of course they knew. But what difference does it make? None. I hear her constantly. She cries at night, in my dreams and in the morning I hear her voice, not a voice, but sounds, dreadful sounds, her blood was gurgling, her blood was speaking. It was maybe calling me, telling me …

GIRL: Yes, you heard her, if you came out of your room.

HUSSEIN: I never said it out loud until now, but I do miss her. My years in prison are a little thing compared to the infinite sadness that I carry in my heart. Her voice sometimes returns and fills the space. I told you. Those who kill must know something about hell that we can't figure out. But sometimes I wonder, do people really die? She haunts me. I think that those who die violently refuse to disappear. They linger around … They beg for their peace, probably. We breathe them. They take our lives over. There's no escape. No, she is not gone, she is cursing us. I can hear her.

GIRL: All this is behind you Hussein. You don't deserve all this hurt. You need a rest, a new life.

HUSSEIN: I will miss you too one day as much as I miss her, if not more. No new life without you.

GIRL: I love you Hussein, I love you … But we'll never live together, I can't tell you why … it's not my fault. I'm in a prison too, somehow. My Mother watches, she has to be informed on everything, I can't look at a flower that she doesn't make a comment. I feel as if she were sitting in my head. It's dreadful.

HUSSEIN: When I met you it was like the moment when I came out from prison. I saw the daylight, and it was too strong for my eyes, much too strong. In every sense of the word, prison is obscurity, and that light everywhere outside terrified me. And when I saw you for the first time, that terror came back, that beneficial terror. That light, I'm telling you, I saw it return. It was you. You gave the world back to me.

GIRL: You must forget, Hussein, forget the misery. But I'm bringing you trouble too. One day, I'll pay you the money I owe you, although I don't know how. But I thank you, oh I thank you.

HUSSEIN: If only you loved me ... you don't need to thank me.

GIRL: I'm sorry. In my own ways ... But I repeat, the idea to commit myself to a marriage is unbearable ... I need space, I need time, I just can't.

HUSSEIN: I am not mad at your Mother although she hurt me deeply ... she clarified the confusion in which I am living. The same thing happened probably to my sister that happened to me: when she met that man, whoever he was, she must have seen the light that I saw when I met you for the first time. Love is revelation, I understand now, the most important among all revelations. One doesn't recover from it, and doesn't want to recover. I wish she had been happy, for at least once, one single night. Do I dare to wish that, add sin to sin? But I do, I do, yes, I must, love is no sin … and we killed her.

GIRL: You have a future, Hussein, you must look ahead.

HUSSEIN: You don't get it. Without you, the future will be as bleak as my days now.

GIRL: But there are other things to think about than me!

HUSSEIN: Listen. I should hate your Mother, but I don't. I'm even grateful to her, believe me or not. Our world is rotten, and in her kind of violence there's something good. She thinks clearly. She sees through our excuses, our lies. She's the only one to have sided with my sister. She understood how blood-thirsty the human animal can be, how appealing murder can be to him. She opened my eyes and they will stay open.

GIRL: So you forgive her.

HUSSEIN: It has nothing to do with forgiveness. That's non-sense. She went to the heart of the matter. We have criminal instincts, and anything can trigger them. I paid for what they have done to my sister. I am the one who paid. At least some-body paid. Somebody had to.

GIRL: I wish it weren't you.

HUSSEIN: That's beside the point. I am happy it was me, because I loved her. Maybe she found her peace because of my imprisonment.

GIRL: Don't say that!

HUSSEIN: Yes, I will. But on the other hand your Mother humiliated me in front of all our colleagues. They were already aloof, avoiding me as much as they could. You know it. I always sit alone at a table in the cafeteria. You all chat together and I sit alone, always by myself. You see, by killing her they brought a malediction on all of us, the whole family. We are cursed.

GIRL: Today I will sit with you. I will show to all that you're my friend.

HUSSEIN: You're an angel. You can sit with me if you want. I will be the happiest that I have ever been. But I am serious. I can't stay in this place from now on. Oh, I will keep my word, I will send the money to your Mother, month after month. But I will look for another job. Or go away from this country and find my place somewhere, near or far, it won't matter. I will never see you again, whatever happens, although nothing, really, interests me besides you. It seems that we're not meant to live together. I repeat, everything else is of no importance. I will change prisons, that's all.

GIRL: I'm sorry, Hussein, I'm sorry.

Tolerance (A Monologue)

And the old man stood, and picked up his gun, thunder rolled in the sky. His eyes fixed the garden's distant barrier and saw his enemy—a young man. He took his gun, cold metal in cold hands, "the gun is heavy," he said, "but it will do." His lips travelled eagerly on the metallic tube, he spat, he kissed again. His hands trembled. The sky broke apart, but it wasn't rain that descended, it has his own joy. He said: "murder is my land."

"It's feast day today," he said, "I'm going to kill. The bullet will travel at light's speed and go straight into his brain. You will all see him fall, and like kitchen water, thick and gooey, his brain will fall on top of his head, and I will utter my greatest song of victory. O dark light that will contain the rest of my life, you will bathe me like my mother did at the moment of my birth. I will bathe and swim in his blood. I will annihilate the bastard that dared make courtship to my daughter, that pupil of my eye."

"Look at them! She's with him. Oh God, she found a way to join him. I will have to kill her too, but oh no, she's blood of my blood, the only thing which is really mine, the only one on Earth. He's trying to snatch her from me, and he's a stranger, a son of a bitch. They come from far, like termites. They will eat up Greece, then spread into Europe, like cancer. The boats keep coming, filled with them, birds of ill omen. They arrive like swarms of bees, and they sting. I will start by burning his brain with a single bullet, then we'll take care of the others."

"Straight ahead, look, he's coming. Trees are hiding him, no, he's emerging, the bastard will soon be in full view, I'll get him, I will dispatch him straight into his destiny, on this land of Greece. If my God won't help me, I'll call the gods of this ancient land, my land, to come to my rescue. He's relatively far, I must not miss him. One bullet, I said, for one head. The gods are coming. I'm hearing them. They will hold my arm, move my fingers, release the bullet, and from there on the world will be cleaner. Will resurrect. Others will do like I do, for the bastards are plenty. I'm ready."

"Oh God, he's as black as a raven just out of the Deluge. He's polluting my garden. I would rather see a snake than see him crawl by the fence. My fence."

"I hear voices. He's talking. Talking to my daughter. She loves him. If only it weren't true! But it is. He dares come to my country, then sets his eyes on my innocent girl. Let no one tell me that she loves this monster, this malediction."

"He's moving, walking carefully, talking. I'll blow his brains out of his skull, blow out his guts. Here he is, here, in clear view. I am firing, one shot, two shots, to make sure that I got him, oh God, he's down, down, he's a bundle, a shadow!"

"He's nothing! But what am I seeing? Another body? A white dress? Would it be my daughter? Do I see it well? Could it be? Yes, it is. I fired two shots, to make sure the bastard is reached. And the second shot was sheer evil, I killed my daughter. O to howl like a wolf! Daughter, you have an animal in me, not a father."

"I am never going to be a human being again, never. By killing the stranger I killed my own flesh. People of Greece, look, I am a murderer, there's no use for me to go on being alive."

"Here I am, standing over two dead bodies. My enemy's, and my child's. I united them in a same sleep. I married them in death. What should I do? What should I think? What have I spilled? Blood on my land, blood of my blood."

"Here they are, united by my own fury. Nothing will now ever separate them, because they are no more. They gave to each other their own souls, I prevented them to join hands. That's what I did."

"And is that what all of us will do forever, kill one foreigner after another, to a saturation point? Are we going to turn the sea, mother of Greece, into a pool of blood, and the soil I'm speaking on into an endless cemetery?"

"Nooooo! A huge beam of light is descending, it's blinding me. I hear sounds. They spring from Earth's deep center. It's my daughter's voice, mixed with his voice. They're trying to say something. I got it. I hear them. From the lower world they're pointing at me. 'Father,' she says, 'you will have to live with what you have done.' And I agree. I am telling you, daughter of mine, my eye's eye, there's nothing good in hatred. It leads to the amputation of one's own soul, it leads to murder! It has no future."

"I am standing over two corpses. The one I loved, and the one I hated. Love and hate are the two faces of the same despair: our incapacity to open our heart to all winds. Let the wind blow. Let it enter within the deepest part of my body, let it come and bring fire and burn me. The fire is eating at me, and I want things to stay the way they are now: an old man crying over not one corpse but two, these two inseparable bodies. I will not break the malediction that fell on my head. I will not divide this garden, will not divide my mind, will not mourn the one and not the other."

"I see in this full light something I never saw before: but there's a paradise made of love. These lovers are already in it. O God forgive me! O Panaïa talk to me. I am so alone. Abandoned to my sorrow. But I will not cry. I am still a man. God, as you forgive, I will forgive. Though I am not religious, I'm discovering a common humanity between me and the man I just killed. This miserable foreigner had in his head the dreams I myself had when I was young, and as impatient as a horse. I smothered his future. Yes, I did, and what's left for me is blood on my hands. He was like I was, a dreamer wanting a better life, same desires, same pains. And what did I do to her, the one I used to call the light of my life, what did I do, I killed her too."

"Now, I will bury them with my own hands, in this little corner, to let them sleep in peace. I want, I want, if they could hear me, I want to bless them. I want to kiss my daughter goodbye, giving her my peace. As for him, I want to love him, if that's possible, yes, I want to love him—I want a new sun on this tired land."

A Library Set on Fire

Lines running in all directions, silence, displacements, verticals turning, rotating, manuscripts burning, each flame annihilating a word, then a sentence, unread and unpublished secrets, leaps of thought, discoveries immaterial although laid on paper, logarithms, recorded conversations between people long since dead, exchanges of anger, of nocturnal flights, discoveries made by the imagination within imagination's boundless boundaries, measurements of planetary motions and locations, within their ephemeral nature, sequences of political theories pitted against rulers, physical desires transformed into divine love, adultery and chastity at war, blood looking for arteries made of clay, the fire eating old brains from the past, the deconstructing of civilization, al-Hallaj running wild through the fire proclaiming "I am God" over any standing loudspeaker, with his toes, his nails and his hair catching fire, all this made forever unknown by the rape of Baghdad an April day when the Tigris was pregnant with apprehension and dreading its merger with the betraying waters of the Gulf.

Angels, More Angels

As children we were told that we have a guardian angel just behind our right shoulder and a bad angel behind the left one. This used to puzzle me. I used to turn my head to the right, to try to see the good angel, but he would never appear. On the left side, I wouldn't dare look, afraid to see the negative one. When I was around four years old, on a Palm Sunday, I happened to wander into a nearby church, and the priest fixed wings on my back, which dressed me up as an angel, and I led the neighborhood procession in the streets, and my mother was trying to find me. When at last she found me, she ran toward me and I told her "do not touch me, I am an angel," and she cried.

Ever since, angels have visited me on and off: their nature changed over the years, they haunted me, or disappeared for a while. When I started painting, they reappeared through Rilke's *Elegies*, then through Paul Klee's angels. I had one of Klee's angels look over my right shoulder for years. Sometimes that angel would ask me to help him figure out what he was made of, who he was. I was aware of that.

Recently, I was meditating on Einar Schleef's creative genius, on his work for the stage, and angels started visiting me in the form of sounds, rain, mountains, or oceans. I came back to Klee. He had been their catalyst. He had searched for their multiple definitions. There was an avalanche of them, all of them prophetic and terrified. Klee pursued a battle with them, like Delacroix had done in his own ways on the walls of a chapel inside the Saint-Sulpice church in Paris.

I am inclined to think that we are mutable, and that by moments human beings become angels, and then return to their habitual selves.

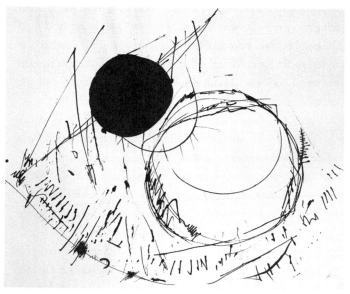

HyperSpace, 1964. Ink on paper

There

This selection is excerpted from the opening pages of the full-length work *There: In the Light and the Darkness of the Self and of the Other*.

Where are we? where? There is a *where*, because we are, stubbornly, and have been, and who are we, if not you and me?

Where are we? Out of History, of his or her story, and back into it, out in Space and back to Earth, out of the womb, and then into dust, who are we?

Where is where, where the terror, the love, the pain? Where the hatred? Where your life, and mine?

There is where, connected to telephone lines, a place for waiting, another for sleeping, a kiss and a flower, and where are we when you are, and where are you when I wait for you to be, be the people I see.

Who are we, a race, a tribe, a herd, a passing phenomenon, or a traveller still travelling in order to find out who we are, and who we shall be?

Are we travelling on a rope, is cancer eating our neighbors, where the sun when night descends, and where paradise on the ocean's asphalt roads?

Who are we, a woman or a man, and is that seasonal, is it eternal, and is it true that there are men and women and it must be true, because you are and I am.

Is there hatred in your heart, and does it mean that I am not here, and where are you when it's getting late?

To go, be going, straight ahead, the world being round, to be coming back, to where, to what, to be a bouncing ball, where, on what, to be defeated by gravity.

Who are you when you're not me, and who am I? Should we be people or fish, sharks, intelligent enough to wipe ourselves off the face of the Earth?

And what is Earth? Some mud, some glue, a meteor, can it belong to itself?

Should you love me because I'm free, and should I follow your destiny instead of mine, out of History, away from Time and its satellites whose names are fear and death? Should I be?

Where are we? In the middle, at the beginning, the end? Who is we, is it you plus me, or something else expandable, explosive, the salt and pepper of our thoughts, the something that may outlast our divinities?

Am I always going by boat, and wherefrom? Am I crying, and why? Are the roads blocked by angels or by soldiers?

I'm asking you to run ahead of yourself and tell me why my bones are cold, or am I wanting you to leave my trees alone and search for water where the rivers overflow?

Going, into a train and stopping nowhere, because *it is* nowhere, with people pouring in, like ripped bags of wheat, birds helplessly flying overhead.

Who are we, us the children of History, whose, which period, which side of History, the wars or the poems, the queens or the strangers, on which side of whose History are we going to be? Are we going to be?

Where are we? In a desert, on a glacier, within a mother's womb or in a woman's eyes, in a man's yearning, or are we into each other, each other's future, as we have been in the past? Are we dead or alive?

I have never been here, where a pleasure boat rocks in the heat, and you have never been in my aunt's garden, where have you been then? We went out to look for you and you were sleeping by a fountain. Where was the moonlight? Where the anguish?

I threw my memories out the window and they came back, alien, beggars and witches, leaving me standing like a sword. Is that why the sun is so bleak when it looks at us, and why is there so much love under the heat and the truth?

Poet of the Here and Now

KLAUDIA RUSCHKOWSKI

It was in spring 1996 that I came to know Etel Adnan. I started reading her poetry and it seized me. I remained overwhelmed by it, by the power and sensitivity of her thinking and writing. It entered my life. It took me like a wave and brought me to a new shore. And this intense experience never stopped, but grows, day by day. Adnan opens up worlds of reflection. She throws light and thought on the various states of the world and of the mind, through her alert perception transformed into poetry. Poetry as a condensed, concentrated form of dealing with presences—with persons and things present, with mental states, and with phenomena—in both philosophical and political ways.

Adnan has the energy to give expression to the smallest things, which one overlooks so easily, and to the most complex facts that determine our lives. Even more, I truly feel that she herself is one of those energies that pervade the world. Her thinking enters its texture, making it tangible. Perhaps it's because of her immense inner freedom, a kind of intrinsic ontological openness. Or it's because of some fixed points in her life beyond the human sphere. Especially, a mountain. For fifty years, she lived opposite Mount Tamalpais, in Marin County, watching it changing with every passing cloud, with every ray of light, flight of birds or drop of rain. Not to speak of its cosmic alliances.

In Beirut, during her childhood, she first found one of her fixed points in the perpetual motion of the sea. She was allowed to swim—for a girl, at that time, unusual. Anyway, she describes herself as an unintentional pioneer, a lifelong one, in many things. And as an alchemical product, with two religions, two languages, two civilizations: the Islamic from her father's side and the Greek from her mother's. The cosmopolitan milieu of the seaport where she grew up, enriched, I suppose, her passionately encompassing view. All the natural phenomena that surrounded her, and which she observed and lived with, contributed to her spirit's nomadic essence. This nomadism is what essentially characterizes her work. Like Nietzsche, her most beloved philosopher—by the way, she understands him to be a poet—Adnan seems to me a "rendez-vous of experiences" *de toutes les couleurs*. Love is surely at the core of them, most certainly red.

Love prevails, despite the many catastrophes she has had to live through, and the determining experiences of loss. Her mother lost Smyrna, her native city, in the great fire of 1922. Her father lost the Ottoman Empire, where he was a General Staff officer. That means, he lost his world. Adnan herself lost the Beirut that she loved, in the civil war that burst forth in 1975. With *The Arab Apocalypse*, a series of fifty-nine poems that is one of her major works, first published in Paris, in 1980, she presented a fierce political, cultural, and social critique of an eruption of blind violence and devastating power plays that, in the end, led to fifteen years of war. An Apocalypse, not only for Lebanon but for the whole Arab World. Into those poems she inserted little signs or scribbles, the surplus of emotion, even the unimaginable, the unsaid. Thus, she created powerful visual-semantic fields describing physical assault and psychic damage.

She has worked with signs since the early sixties, when she created her first *leporellos*, folding books that are particularly dear to her because they combine poetry and art. Their inherent permanent becoming and constant transformation correspond perfectly to her spiritual fluidity, to her curiosity about discoveries and the unforeseeable. Moreover, they helped her recognize painting as a language that can go as far as any other language. Maybe even farther, because it transgresses linguistic borders. Adnan's writing is very much involved with history, it makes things visible. Her painting expresses her profound affection for the world, for nature and its forces, it reveals her happiness to exist. She herself describes it beautifully: "I write what I see, I paint what I am."

I am fascinated by her confidence that, in any circumstance, the essence of what she wants to express will emerge. This trust in the process of creating provides liberty. While reading, and, more so, translating her poetry, I feel it deeply. The inherent philosophical concepts that shine through the lines sometimes work as crucial points for catching a swarm of thoughts, or as a springboard for hopping off to audacious inferences, never being intrusive. Admirable are her open dialogues with Nietzsche, Hegel or Heidegger. Nietzsche, as she sees it, destroyed our faith in classical philosophy. And it was Heidegger who made it clear that Hölderlin was perhaps more of a philosopher than poet. What attracts her is the kind of open philosophy that renounces the search for truth, but rather one that creates contradictions. Like poetry.

Even more, I am thrilled by her intimate conversations with Paul Klee, the painter she fell in love with early, grateful that she allows us to listen, and beyond that, to participate with our own reflections, our own perceptions. Of colors, especially. In the ancient city of Kairouan, Adnan remembers, during his legendary Tunisian journey that changed modern art, Paul Klee wrote: "Color and I are one." She felt that he thought it to be a revelation. Doubtless, it is the same for her. For both artists colors exist as metaphysical beings, the very indications of life. She is convinced that colors are able to perforate time barriers, that they have the power to guide us to universal spaces where the knowledge of life is stored. Einstein reflected on the possibility of riding a beam of light. Adnan rides flying carpets, looking incessantly for the next wave, sure that "there's always a conductive thread through space for an untenable position."

The abundance of her awareness, coupled with the poignancy of her observations and her absolute open-mindedness to life and whatever happens, opens up a universe that Etel Adnan invites us to enter.

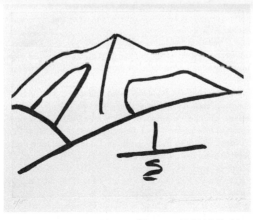

Montagne II, 2015. Etching

List of Images

Books by the Author

Surge

To look at the sea is to become what one is: An Etel Adnan Reader

Night

Premonition

Sea and Fog

The Cost for Love We Are Not Willing to Pay

Master of the Eclipse

Seasons

In the Heart of the Heart of Another Country

In/somnia

There: In the Light and the Darkness of the Self and of the Other

Paris, When It's Naked

Of Cities & Women (Letters To Fawwaz)

The Spring Flowers Own & The Manifestations of the Voyage

The Arab Apocalypse

Journey To Mount Tamalpais

The Indian Never Had A Horse & Other Poems

Sitt Marie-Rose

From A To Z

Five Senses for One Death

Moonshots

About the Author

PHOTO: ANTONIO MARIA STORCH

ETEL ADNAN was born in Beirut in 1925. She left Lebanon in the late 1940s to attend the Sorbonne, and in the next decade she went to the Bay Area to study at the University of California, Berkeley, before moving to Sausalito and taking a teaching position at Dominion College. She returned to Beirut in the early 1970s where she worked as cultural editor of French-language newspapers, until the Lebanese Civil War forced her to leave the country. Adnan eventually made her home in Sausalito for many years, with frequent travels abroad. She now resides in Paris.

As an admired author, she has received many awards for her more than fifteen books: France Pays-Arab Award, PEN Oakland Josephine Miles Book Award, Arab American Book Award, California Book Award for Poetry, Small Press Traffic Lifetime Achievement Award, Lambda Literary Award for Lesbian Poetry, and Lifetime Achievement Award from Radius of Arab American Writers. The Etel Adnan Award for Women Playwrights was established by the Al-Medina Theatre of Beirut to support women writers in the Arab World. Her poems, plays, and literary texts have been performed or adapted for theatre, opera, and radio in the U.S. and Europe. Robert Wilson invited her to write the French section of his multicountry opera, *the CIVIL warS: a tree is best measured when it is down*, in 1984. Etel Adnan was honored with France's L'Ordre de Chevalier des Arts in 2014.

Adnan's paintings, drawings, fold-out books, ceramics, and tapestries are exhibited on several continents, with recent solo shows at the Irish Museum of Modern Art (Dublin); Museum der Moderne Salzburg; Mathaf: Arab Museum of Modern Art (Doha); dOCUMENTA (13) (Kassel); MASS MoCA (North Adams, MA); Zentrum Paul Klee (Bern); San Francisco Museum of Modern Art. Etel Adnan is represented by Galerie Lelong, Paris and New York.

About the Editors

BONNIE MARRANCA is founding editor and publisher of PAJ Publications/*PAJ: A Journal of Performance and Art*. She is the author of *Performance Histories, Ecologies of Theatre*, and *Theatrewritings*. She has also edited several collections of essays, interviews, and plays, including *Conversations with Meredith Monk, New Europe: plays from the continent, Plays for the End of the Century*, and *Conversations on Art and Performance*. A Guggenheim Fellow and Fulbright Scholar, she has also received the Leverhulme Trust Visiting Professorship (UK), Asian Cultural Council Fellowship (Japan), and Anschutz Distinguished Fellowship in American Studies (Princeton University). She has lectured and taught widely in American and European universities, and is Professor of Theatre at The New School/Eugene Lang College of Liberal Arts.

KLAUDIA RUSCHKOWSKI is an author, curator, editor, and translator, who has also worked as a dramaturg in German theatres. She co-founded/co-directed the European Culture Center of Thuringia, and held the position of associate editor of *Via Regia*, an international journal for cultural communication. For several years, she conceived programs on the playwright Heiner Müller, and served as associate editor of German publications of his plays. Her activities include curating exhibitions, literary and translation projects, and radio plays for which she received several award nominations. For more than two decades, she has collaborated with Etel Adnan in translating into German her poetry volumes *Seasons, Sea and Fog, Conversations with My Soul*, and *Night*, as well as organizing performances and exhibitions on *The Arab Apocalypse* and *Night*. She lives in Volterra, Italy.